## Disclaimer

This book is intended for informational and educational purposes only. The authors, editors, and publishers have made every effort to ensure the accuracy and completeness of the information contained herein. However, the rapidly evolving nature of the cryptocurrency and blockchain sectors, along with the inherent risks associated with digital assets and their underlying technologies, means that details, interpretations, and best practices can change over time.

Neither the authors nor the publishers assume any liability or responsibility for any errors or omissions. No information in this book should be interpreted as financial, investment, legal, or tax advice. Readers are strongly advised to consult with appropriate professionals in the respective fields before making any decisions based on the content of this book.

Any investment in cryptocurrency or engagement with blockchain technology carries inherent risks, and past performance does not guarantee future results. Always conduct thorough research and exercise due diligence.

Mentions of specific companies, platforms, products, or services are for illustrative purposes only and do not constitute endorsements. The views and opinions expressed in this book are those of the authors and do not necessarily reflect the official policy or position of any other agency, organization, or company.

By continuing to read this book, the reader acknowledges the above terms and assumes all responsibility for any actions taken based on the content of this book.

# Crypto Bites: Snack-sized Insights for the Modern Investor

## Introduction: Journeying Through the Digital Odyssey

As we cast our eyes back on the tapestry of financial evolution, few chapters are as transformative as the advent of cryptocurrency and blockchain technology. Beginning in 2008 with an enigmatic white paper by Satoshi Nakamoto titled "Bitcoin: A Peer-to-Peer Electronic Cash System," this domain has exponentially expanded into a vast galaxy comprising a myriad of tokens, intelligent contracts, decentralized platforms, and beyond. Through the lens of this book, we aim to illuminate the pathways of this ever-evolving digital odyssey.

Bitcoin's stratospheric ascent undoubtedly captured the world's attention. Still, the real marvel was its underpinning backbone – the blockchain. This ingenious decentralized ledger, conceived initially to bolster Bitcoin, has since unfurled its wings, showcasing applications that transcend the realm of digital currencies. Its touch is seen from transforming global supply chains to pioneering a new era in finance.

However, akin to all frontiers, the crypto universe is a blend of golden prospects interspersed with treacherous quicksands. Tales of unprecedented success are paralleled by stories of grievous misadventures. It is a domain that demands astute navigation.

To enhance your journey, we recommend platforms like CryptoWisdom.com. Renowned for offering in-depth courses, insightful crypto training videos, literature, and more, it can serve as a lighthouse in the vast ocean of crypto knowledge.

Whether you're a seasoned crypto enthusiast, a conventional investor peering into this digital realm, or a novice grappling with jargons like "DeFi" or "NFT," this tome is your compass. We voyage from the bedrock principles, diving into the intricate mechanics, opportunities, challenges, and envisioning what the horizon might hold.

As you flip to the ensuing pages, realize that this isn't merely an exploration of technological marvel but a leap into a revolutionary epoch. Blockchain's decentralized ethos challenges age-old tenets of authority, autonomy, and faith. Though the horizon remains shrouded in mist, acquainting oneself with the map is the inaugural step of this magnificent expedition.

So, as you stand at the cusp of this digital realm, we extend our hand. Join us on this enlightening quest, charting the uncharted, and unraveling the mysteries of cryptocurrency.

This book is part of the Crypto Wisdom digital asset education series:
www.CryptoWisdom.com

# Crypto Bites: Snack-sized Insights for the Modern Investor

## Contents

# Crypto Bites: Snack-sized Insights for the Modern Investor

# Crypto Bites: Snack-sized Insights for the Modern Investor

Chapter 1: The Basics of Cryptocurrencies

Origin and Philosophy

Cryptocurrencies, in essence, are digital or virtual currencies that utilize cryptography for security, making them resistant to counterfeit. Their decentralized nature sets them apart from traditional currencies.

The concept of cryptocurrencies was popularized by Bitcoin, the pioneering digital currency introduced by an anonymous entity called Satoshi Nakamoto in 2008. Nakamoto released a whitepaper titled "Bitcoin: A Peer-to-Peer Electronic Cash System," delineating the idea of creating a decentralized digital currency that operates without a central authority or single administrator. Transactions occur directly between users and are verified via network nodes through cryptography.

Behind this innovation was a deeper philosophy. Nakamoto's intent was not just to create a new currency. The decentralized nature of Bitcoin was a direct response to the 2008 financial crisis, highlighting issues of trust in traditional banking systems and central authorities. By ensuring that transactions are irreversible and don't rely on a central entity, the decentralized system eliminates the need for trust in big institutions. Bitcoin's decentralization represents a shift from trust in people to trust in technology.

Cryptocurrencies, with Bitcoin at the forefront, present a revolutionary approach to finance. They challenge traditional monetary systems and introduce a paradigm where power isn't held by a few central entities but is distributed across a network.

# Crypto Bites: Snack-sized Insights for the Modern Investor

What is Blockchain?: Understanding the Foundational Technology Behind Most Cryptocurrencies:

The term "blockchain" often conjures images of complex algorithms and cryptographic jargon. At its core, however, the concept is elegantly simple. Blockchain is, in essence, a digital ledger. Imagine a book where you record every transaction you make. Now, envision thousands of people having the same book, and whenever a transaction occurs, everyone updates their copy. This shared and synchronized ledger is the basic idea behind a blockchain.

Each "block" in the blockchain contains a number of transactions. When a block is "completed" or "filled" with transactions, a new block is created and linked to the previous, forming a chain. This chain of blocks ensures a chronological and immutable record of transactions.

The revolutionary aspect of blockchain is its decentralized nature. Traditional databases, like a SQL database, have a central entity overseeing and validating transactions. Blockchains, on the other hand, distribute this responsibility among numerous participants in the network, known as nodes. Each node possesses a copy of the entire blockchain and works collectively to validate and record new transactions. When a transaction occurs, it must be approved by a majority of nodes, ensuring transparency and reducing the potential for fraud.

Moreover, once a block is added to the blockchain, its content becomes unchangeable, adding a layer of security and trust to the data. This immutability arises from cryptographic functions ensuring that any alteration to a block would break the continuity of the chain.

In sum, blockchain is the backbone of cryptocurrencies, ensuring decentralized, transparent, and secure transactions in the digital realm.

Notes: _____

_____

_____

# Crypto Bites: Snack-sized Insights for the Modern Investor

How Transactions Work : From Initiation to Validation and Confirmation on the Blockchain

At its core, a cryptocurrency transaction is a digital exchange of value, facilitated by the underlying blockchain technology. Here's a step-by-step breakdown of how these transactions typically progress:

1. Initiation: It begins when someone, say Alice, wants to send a unit of cryptocurrency to Bob. Alice initiates the transaction using a digital wallet, specifying Bob's wallet address and the amount she wishes to transfer.
2. Transaction Creation: The transaction details, including the sender's and receiver's wallet addresses and the amount, are combined to create a digital 'package'. This package is also signed with Alice's private key, a unique cryptographic identifier.
3. Broadcast: This digital package, now known as a transaction, is broadcast to the cryptocurrency network, reaching nodes or participants in the network.
4. Validation: Before a transaction is confirmed, it must be validated. Nodes in the network use algorithms to verify the transaction's legitimacy. They check if Alice has the necessary funds and if her digital signature matches, ensuring she's the rightful owner.
5. Mining: Transactions waiting for confirmation are picked up by miners (in Proof of Work systems). Miners solve complex mathematical problems, and the first to solve it gets to add a new block (containing several transactions) to the blockchain.
6. Confirmation: Once the block is added to the chain, the transaction is considered confirmed. With each subsequent block added after this, the transaction becomes more secure. Typically, a transaction is seen as final after 6 blocks in the Bitcoin network.

In essence, a cryptocurrency transaction travels from initiation through a network of checks and balances, ensuring security and transparency before its final confirmation on the blockchain.

Notes: _____

_____

_____

# Crypto Bites: Snack-sized Insights for the Modern Investor

Mining and Consensus Mechanisms: Verification of Transactions and Block Addition

In the realm of cryptocurrencies, "mining" and "consensus mechanisms" are foundational concepts ensuring the authenticity and security of transactions.

1. Mining: Mining is the process by which new blocks (containing transactions) are added to the blockchain. Miners use powerful computers to solve complex mathematical problems. The first miner to solve the problem gets to add the next block and is rewarded with newly minted (or "mined") cryptocurrency. This serves two purposes: it issues new coins in a decentralized manner and incentivizes individuals to spend computational resources to keep the network secure.
2. Consensus Mechanisms: Before a block is added to the blockchain, there needs to be consensus or agreement within the network that the transactions in the block are valid. This agreement is achieved through consensus mechanisms.
   - Proof of Work (PoW): This is the original consensus mechanism adopted by Bitcoin. In PoW, miners compete to solve a cryptographic puzzle. The first to solve it gets to add the next block. However, PoW is criticized for its environmental impact, as it requires immense computational power and energy.
   - Proof of Stake (PoS): As an alternative to PoW, PoS was introduced to address environmental concerns. In PoS, validators (or participants) are chosen to create new blocks based on the number of coins they hold and are willing to "stake" or lock up as collateral. It's seen as a more energy-efficient alternative to PoW.

In essence, mining and consensus mechanisms form the backbone of cryptocurrency networks, ensuring that transactions are authenticated, and the blockchain remains secure and tamper-proof.

Notes: _____

_____

_____

# Crypto Bites: Snack-sized Insights for the Modern Investor

Public and Private Keys: Cryptographic Pillars of Cryptocurrency Security

Cryptocurrencies operate within the realm of cryptography, ensuring the security and privacy of transactions. Two of the most fundamental cryptographic components are the public and private keys, acting as the linchpin for securing ownership and validating transactions.

1. Private Key: Think of the private key as a highly guarded secret password. It's a lengthy, unique string of alphanumeric characters known only to the owner. The private key is instrumental in creating digital signatures for transactions. Essentially, when you want to send cryptocurrency, you sign the transaction with your private key, proving ownership. It's of paramount importance to keep this key confidential. If someone else gains access to your private key, they gain control over your cryptocurrency holdings.

2. Public Key: Derived from the private key through a mathematical algorithm, the public key, as its name suggests, is publicly accessible. It can be compared to an email address that you share with others. When someone wants to send you cryptocurrency, they send it to your public key. However, unlike an email, the public key and its corresponding cryptocurrency holdings remain secure, as one needs the private key to access and spend those funds.

3. Digital Signatures: When initiating a transaction, the sender's private key and the transaction details are used to create a digital signature. This signature is then verified by others in the network using the sender's public key, ensuring the transaction's authenticity without revealing the private key.

In the intricate dance of cryptocurrency transactions, the private and public keys ensure a symphony of security, authentication, and privacy.

Notes: _____

_____

_____

Digital Wallets: Storing Cryptocurrencies Securely and Efficiently

In the world of cryptocurrencies, digital wallets play a crucial role as they provide a secure place to store, send, and receive digital assets. These wallets don't store coins per se; instead, they store cryptographic keys (public and private) that grant ownership and access to the coins on the blockchain.

1. Hot Wallets: Think of these as online wallets. They are constantly connected to the internet, making them easily accessible and user-friendly. Examples include web wallets, mobile wallets, and desktop wallets. While they provide convenience, especially for frequent transactions, their always-online nature makes them vulnerable to cyber-attacks, hacks, and malware.
2. Cold Wallets: Opposite to hot wallets, cold wallets are offline, providing an added layer of security. Since they're not constantly connected to the internet, they're immune to online hacks. They're particularly suitable for storing large amounts of cryptocurrency over extended periods. Paper wallets, where the public and private keys are printed on paper, are an example of cold storage.
3. Hardware Wallets: A hardware wallet is a physical electronic device resembling a USB stick. It's designed to securely generate and store a user's private keys offline. Transactions can be initiated online, but they're signed offline within the device, ensuring the private key never exposes itself to online vulnerabilities.

In conclusion, the choice of a digital wallet depends on the user's needs. For frequent access and transactions, hot wallets are ideal, but for long-term, secure holding, cold and hardware wallets offer superior protection.

Notes: _____

_____

_____

# Crypto Bites: Snack-sized Insights for the Modern Investor

Decentralization vs. Centralization: Contrasting New Age Systems with Traditional Financial Constructs

In the context of finance and technology, centralization and decentralization refer to the distribution of authority and control within a system. The advent of cryptocurrencies brought to the fore a paradigm shift from conventional centralized mechanisms to decentralized networks.

1. Centralization: Centralized systems are characterized by a single authority or entity that holds predominant power and control. Traditional banking is a prime example. Here, the bank controls your money, manages transactions, and has the authority to freeze assets or implement policies. Centralization can lead to efficiency, as there's a singular point of control, but it also becomes a single point of failure and subjects participants to the whims and vulnerabilities of that central entity.

2. Decentralization: Decentralized systems operate on a peer-to-peer basis without a central authority. Cryptocurrencies like Bitcoin epitomize this, where transactions happen directly between users, and a distributed ledger (blockchain) verifies them. Decentralization imparts:
   - Security: No single point of failure, reducing vulnerability to centralized attacks or system failures.
   - Empowerment: Participants have full control over their assets.
   - Transparency: Open-source nature ensures everyone can verify transactions.
   - Censorship-resistance: Harder to regulate or control by any single entity or government.

3. Significance: The move toward decentralization in the financial realm challenges existing power structures. While centralized systems have provided structure and order for years, they've also been plagued by inefficiencies, bureaucratic red tape, and exclusions. Decentralization offers a more inclusive, transparent, and empowering alternative.

In essence, while centralization centralizes trust and power, decentralization distributes it, leading to a more democratized and resilient system.

Notes: _____

_____

_____

# Crypto Bites: Snack-sized Insights for the Modern Investor

Understanding Cryptocurrency Value: Unpacking the Dynamics of Valuation

Cryptocurrencies, unlike traditional currencies, aren't backed by physical commodities like gold or the decree of a central authority. So, what then determines their value? A confluence of factors comes into play:

1. Supply and Demand: Just as with any commodity, the basic economic principles of supply and demand largely influence the value of cryptocurrencies. If a cryptocurrency has a high token supply with little demand from traders and users, its value will drop. Conversely, if the supply of a particular cryptocurrency is limited and the demand is high, then its value can rise significantly.
2. Utility: The value of a cryptocurrency also depends on how functional and useful it is. Can you use the token to real-world applications? For instance, Ethereum can be used to execute smart contracts on its platform, thereby providing it with intrinsic utility and value.
3. Scarcity: Bitcoin is a prime example when discussing scarcity. Its total supply is capped at 21 million coins, fostering a degree of scarcity. This limited supply ensures that inflation doesn't devalue Bitcoins. The more scarce the cryptocurrency, the higher the potential value.
4. Perceived Value: Just as with any other asset, perception is critical in determining the value of a cryptocurrency. News events, public sentiment, technological advancements, and market manipulation can influence people's perception and, in turn, drive demand and value.

In essence, while intrinsic factors like utility and scarcity play a role, the value of cryptocurrencies is also a reflection of the trust and belief people place in them. Just like gold or fiat money, if people perceive value in it, it becomes valuable.

Notes: _____

_____

_____

# Crypto Bites: Snack-sized Insights for the Modern Investor

Altcoins and the Broader Crypto Ecosystem: Venturing Beyond Bitcoin

While Bitcoin holds the title of the inaugural and most recognized cryptocurrency, the crypto ecosystem has burgeoned to include a vast array of alternative coins, colloquially termed "altcoins". These altcoins have emerged with varied purposes, features, and technologies:

1. What are Altcoins?: The term 'altcoin' is derived from two words: 'alternative' and 'coin'. Essentially, any cryptocurrency other than Bitcoin is categorized as an altcoin. As of now, there are thousands of them, each trying to carve a niche or present a new solution.
2. Types of Altcoins:
    o Forked from Bitcoin: Some altcoins are derived from Bitcoin's open-source protocol. Examples include Bitcoin Cash and Bitcoin SV, which were born from disagreements within the Bitcoin community about its direction.
    o Native Blockchain Platforms: Altcoins like Ethereum and Cardano have their unique blockchains and bring innovative functionalities, such as smart contracts.
    o Stablecoins: Tether (USDT) and USD Coin (USDC) are pegged to traditional fiat currencies, striving for price stability.
    o Privacy Coins: Monero and Zcash prioritize transaction privacy and anonymity beyond what Bitcoin offers.
3. Significance: Altcoins often propose improvements, alternatives, or expansions to Bitcoin's limitations. Ethereum's smart contracts, for instance, pave the way for decentralized applications (dApps). Meanwhile, stablecoins aim to meld the benefits of cryptocurrencies with the stability of fiat.
4. Investor Note: While the altcoin universe brims with innovation, it's essential to approach with caution. Many altcoins are experimental, and their value can be more volatile than Bitcoin.

In conclusion, the crypto ecosystem is not monolithic. Beyond Bitcoin lies a vast and varied altcoin landscape, rich in potential but also fraught with risk.

Notes: _____

_____

_____

# Crypto Bites: Snack-sized Insights for the Modern Investor

History of Cryptocurrency Milestones: A Journey from Bitcoin's Inception to the Diverse Crypto Landscape

Cryptocurrency, although a relatively new phenomenon, has experienced significant milestones since its inception. Here's a brief chronology:

1. 2008 - Bitcoin's Whitepaper: The journey commenced when an anonymous entity, Satoshi Nakamoto, released the Bitcoin whitepaper. This document laid the foundation for the first decentralized cryptocurrency.
2. 2009 - Bitcoin's Genesis Block: The first block, known as the 'genesis block', was mined by Satoshi, marking the birth of Bitcoin.
3. 2010 - Bitcoin's First Value Proposition: A developer named Laszlo Hanyecz made the first real-world transaction by buying two pizzas for 10,000 Bitcoins, indirectly establishing a monetary value for the cryptocurrency.
4. 2011 - Rise of Altcoins: With Bitcoin gaining traction, the first altcoins started to emerge. Litecoin, often dubbed 'silver to Bitcoin's gold', was among the pioneers.
5. 2013 - Bitcoin Reaches $1,000: A significant market milestone, Bitcoin's price hit $1,000 for the first time, bringing widespread media attention.
6. 2014 - Mt. Gox Collapse: One of the most significant crypto exchanges, Mt. Gox, went bankrupt after a massive hack, highlighting the risks in the crypto sphere.
7. 2017 - ICO Boom and Market Peak: The year saw a massive influx of Initial Coin Offerings (ICOs) as projects sought crowdfunding via token sales. Bitcoin reached an all-time high of nearly $20,000 in December but was followed by a substantial market correction.
8. 2017-2019 - Forks and Divergence: Disagreements within the Bitcoin community led to forks, creating Bitcoin Cash and later Bitcoin SV. Ethereum also experienced a significant fork leading to Ethereum and Ethereum Classic.
9. 2020 onwards - DeFi and Institutional Adoption: The decentralized finance (DeFi) sector exploded in popularity, and significant institutions began endorsing and investing in cryptocurrencies.

Notes: _____

_____

_____

Chapter 2: The Different Cryptocurrencies

Bitcoin (BTC): The Pioneer Cryptocurrency

Bitcoin, often termed as the "digital gold," stands tall as the progenitor of the cryptocurrency movement. Its inception marked not just the birth of a new currency but a revolutionary shift in the world of finance and trust.

1. Historical Genesis:
   o In 2008, an individual or group under the pseudonym 'Satoshi Nakamoto' introduced Bitcoin through a whitepaper titled "Bitcoin: A Peer-to-Peer Electronic Cash System." The concept was to create a decentralized digital currency devoid of central authority, empowering individuals to transact directly.
2. Core Purpose:
   o Bitcoin's raison d'être was straightforward: a peer-to-peer version of electronic cash allowing online payments without going through a financial institution. This was a direct response to the financial crises and the perceived flaws in the traditional banking system.
3. Distinctive Features:
   o Decentralization: Unlike fiat currencies controlled by governments and banks, Bitcoin operates on a decentralized network of computers.
   o Limited Supply: Capped at 21 million, Bitcoin's scarcity is algorithmically defined, rendering it inflation-resistant.
   o Transparent and Immutable: Bitcoin transactions, recorded on the blockchain, are transparent and cannot be altered, ensuring trustworthiness.
4. Bitcoin as "Digital Gold":
   o Beyond being a medium of exchange, Bitcoin has taken on the role of a store of value, akin to gold. This characterization arises from its scarcity, decentralization, and resistance to censorship, which shields it from geopolitical uncertainties and fiat currency devaluations.

In essence, Bitcoin's groundbreaking technology and philosophy have positioned it at the forefront of the crypto movement. Its blend of decentralization, security, and economic principles underscores its continuing significance in the expanding crypto universe.

Notes: _____

_____

_____

# Crypto Bites: Snack-sized Insights for the Modern Investor

Ethereum (ETH): Beyond Currency - Smart Contracts and dApps

Ethereum, while often placed alongside Bitcoin in discussions, has carved a distinct identity for itself in the blockchain world. It wasn't designed as just another cryptocurrency, but as a platform facilitating decentralized applications and smart contracts.

1. The Genesis of Ethereum:
   o Proposed by the prodigious Vitalik Buterin in late 2013 and launched in 2015, Ethereum emerged as an answer to the limitations of Bitcoin. While Bitcoin was revolutionary, it had a restricted scripting language. Buterin envisioned a platform that would allow more complex and programmable applications to run on a blockchain.
2. Smart Contracts – A Leap Forward:
   o At the heart of Ethereum lies the concept of smart contracts. These are self-executing contracts where the agreement between buyer and seller is written into lines of code. Once conditions are met, actions are automatically triggered, reducing the need for intermediaries and increasing efficiency and trust.
3. dApps - Decentralized Applications:
   o Ethereum ushered in the era of dApps – applications that run on a P2P network of computers rather than a single server. This ensures they are immune to control or interference from a third-party entity. Examples include decentralized exchanges and games.
4. Ethereum Virtual Machine (EVM):
   o The EVM is the runtime environment that facilitates the execution of smart contracts on the Ethereum network. It's Turing-complete, which means it can simulate any computer algorithm, making Ethereum exceptionally adaptable.

While Bitcoin democratized money by decentralizing it, Ethereum further expanded the scope of blockchain technology. By introducing programmability via the EVM, smart contracts, and dApps, Ethereum has transformed the potential applications of blockchain, paving the way for a more decentralized digital ecosystem.

Notes: _____

_____

_____

# Crypto Bites: Snack-sized Insights for the Modern Investor

Ripple (XRP): Bridging Traditional Banking with Crypto

In the world of cryptocurrencies, while many projects sought to revolutionize or replace traditional banking, Ripple took a different approach. Ripple aimed to enhance and streamline existing banking systems, particularly in the realm of cross-border payments.

1. Ripple – The Company and the Protocol:
   o Ripple Labs, the company behind the Ripple protocol, was founded in 2012. Unlike many of its contemporaries, Ripple's focus was clear: create a decentralized platform that allows for efficient money transfers between institutions.
2. XRP – The Digital Asset:
   o XRP is the native digital currency of the Ripple network. Distinct from many cryptocurrencies, XRP isn't mined. All 100 billion XRP tokens were pre-mined, and Ripple Labs releases them systematically. This gives XRP unique environmental advantages, as there's no energy-intensive mining process involved.
3. The Vision of Frictionless Transactions:
   o Ripple's primary aim is to allow banks to send real-time international payments seamlessly. Traditionally, banks rely on systems like SWIFT, which can be slow, taking several days, and are accompanied by high fees. Ripple promises transaction settlements in just seconds and at a fraction of the cost.
4. RippleNet – The Network:
   o This decentralized network of institutional payment providers, such as banks and money services businesses, uses Ripple's technology to facilitate real-time, cross-border payments. RippleNet offers end-to-end tracking, ensuring secure, instantaneous, and low-cost international transactions.

Ripple, with XRP at its helm, is a testament to the potential of blockchain technology in reshaping the global financial infrastructure. Rather than replacing traditional banking, Ripple exemplifies how cryptocurrency and blockchain can be harnessed to enhance and upgrade existing financial systems.

Notes: _____

_____

_____

Litecoin (LTC): The Silver to Bitcoin's Gold

Litecoin, often dubbed the "silver to Bitcoin's gold," emerged as a prominent alternative to Bitcoin in the early days of the cryptocurrency revolution. Created by Charlie Lee in 2011, Litecoin was one of the first forks of the Bitcoin core client. It was designed with a vision to address some of Bitcoin's limitations and offer a complementary crypto solution.

1. Origins and Vision:
   - Charlie Lee, a former Google engineer, saw an opportunity to refine the Bitcoin model. Recognizing the potential bottlenecks and scalability issues Bitcoin might face as it grew, Lee designed Litecoin as a more lightweight version (hence the name) that could facilitate faster and cheaper transactions.
2. Key Differences:
   - Transaction Speed: Litecoin boasts a quicker block generation time, approximately 2.5 minutes, compared to Bitcoin's 10 minutes. This results in faster transaction confirmations.
   - Hashing Algorithm: Unlike Bitcoin's SHA-256 hashing algorithm, Litecoin employs Scrypt. This significant distinction affects the process of mining. Scrypt was chosen to ensure a more democratized mining process, allowing users with regular computers to participate without the need for specialized ASICs.
   - Supply Limit: Litecoin has a maximum supply of 84 million coins, precisely four times Bitcoin's 21 million cap, aligning with its faster transaction rate.
3. Position in the Crypto Ecosystem:
   - Litecoin is not out to replace Bitcoin. Instead, it has carved a niche as a more transaction-friendly alternative, suitable for smaller and more frequent transactions. It's analogous to how silver, being more abundant and cheaper than gold, is often used for smaller, day-to-day monetary exchanges.

Litecoin's development and continued presence underscore the diverse needs and solutions within the crypto ecosystem. By addressing certain perceived limitations of Bitcoin while embracing its foundational principles, Litecoin showcases how the world of digital assets can evolve and adapt.

# Crypto Bites: Snack-sized Insights for the Modern Investor

Emerging Altcoins: From Chainlink, Polygon to Cardano

The cryptocurrency universe extends far beyond Bitcoin and Ethereum. Among the vast array of altcoins (alternative coins to Bitcoin), several have distinguished themselves with unique value propositions, technical innovations, and significant community backing. Two such noteworthy altcoins are Chainlink and Cardano.

1. **Chainlink (LINK)**:
   - *Purpose*: Chainlink serves as a decentralized oracle network. It acts as a bridge, connecting smart contracts on the blockchain with real-world data, APIs, and traditional payment systems. Without such oracles, smart contracts would be limited in their functionality as they can only access data within their respective blockchains.
   - *Unique Proposition*: Chainlink's decentralized nature ensures data integrity and security. By utilizing multiple data sources and node operators, it reduces the risk associated with centralization and single points of failure. The LINK token is used as payment for data services within the ecosystem.
2. **Polygon (MATIC)**:
   - *Purpose*: Originally known as Matic Network, Polygon aims to address some of Ethereum's major limitations, including its throughput, poor UX, and delayed PoS Ethereum transition. It enhances the capacity and reduces the latency of dApps running on platforms like Ethereum.
   - *Unique Proposition*: Polygon is often termed as Ethereum's "Internet of Blockchains". It's a multi-chain scaling solution that offers a framework for building and connecting Ethereum-compatible blockchain networks. The MATIC token is used for transaction fees and staking within the network.
3. **Cardano (ADA)**:
   - *Purpose*: Developed by a team of academicians and engineers, Cardano aspires to be a more secure, scalable, and sustainable blockchain for running smart contracts, similar to Ethereum.
   - *Unique Proposition*: Cardano adopts a research-driven approach, with its design and development grounded in scientific research and formal methods. Its two-layered architecture separates the ledger of account values from the reason why values are moved from one account to the other, ensuring more flexibility and security. The ADA token serves as the network's currency and a means to power its smart contracts.

In summary, while all three altcoins—Chainlink, Polygon, and Cardano—operate within the crypto ecosystem, each offers distinctive solutions addressing specific challenges, from real-world data integration and scalability issues to improved security and sustainability in blockchain operations.

Chapter 3: Token Types

Basics of Fungible Tokens (ERC-20)

ERC-20 tokens have become a foundational building block within the Ethereum ecosystem, serving as a standardized protocol for fungible tokens. Here's a brief overview:

- Definition: "Fungible" means that each token is identical and interchangeable. Think of it like regular currency coins, where every dollar or penny is equal in value to another of its kind.
- Standardization: ERC-20 outlines a set of standardized functions that a token on Ethereum should implement. This includes methods to get the total token supply, retrieve account balances, transfer tokens, and approve third-party transfers. The standard ensures that different applications and wallets can seamlessly interact with any ERC-20 token.
- Applications: Due to their standardized nature, ERC-20 tokens have become the go-to for various crypto-based projects. They've been leveraged extensively in Initial Coin Offerings (ICOs) as a means for projects to raise capital. Moreover, most DeFi projects on Ethereum use ERC-20 tokens either as governance tokens or as assets within their platforms.

In summary, ERC-20 tokens offer a consistent, interchangeable, and versatile means to represent value and utility within the Ethereum blockchain's diverse applications.

Notes: _____

_____

_____

Basics of Non-Fungible Tokens (ERC-721)

Non-Fungible Tokens (NFTs) represent one of the most groundbreaking evolutions in the blockchain world, particularly on the Ethereum platform, which standardized their format via the ERC-721 protocol. Here's a snapshot:

- Uniqueness: Unlike fungible tokens where each unit is identical (like ERC-20 tokens), each NFT is distinct, ensuring individuality and non-interchangeability. This means that one NFT cannot be exchanged on a one-to-one basis with another.
- Properties & Provenance: NFTs can contain rich metadata within their design, providing unique information, attributes, or even stories about the asset they represent. Moreover, their immutability ensures the verification of authenticity and origin - a digital certificate of authenticity.
- Value of Rarity: The singular nature of NFTs has driven their popularity in realms like digital art, collectibles, and even virtual real estate. This rarity, combined with demand, has led to some NFTs fetching astronomical prices, reminiscent of physical art auctions.
- Applications: Beyond art, NFTs are revolutionizing music, gaming, sports, and more by offering unique, verifiable digital ownership in various formats.

In essence, ERC-721 tokens or NFTs have redefined digital ownership, offering a powerful means to digitize and trade singular assets in diverse sectors.

Notes: _____

_____

_____

Utility of Fungible Tokens in the Ecosystem

Fungible tokens, especially when following standards like ERC-20 on the Ethereum blockchain, play a pivotal role in the crypto ecosystem. Let's unpack their multifaceted applications:

- Stablecoins: These are digital assets pegged to the value of a stable entity, like the US Dollar. Fungible tokens represent these stablecoins, ensuring that each token, whether it's USDC, DAI, or Tether, maintains the same value and is interchangeable with another of its kind.
- Governance Tokens: Decentralized platforms often employ fungible tokens as governance tokens, granting holders voting rights. Examples include COMP from Compound or UNI from Uniswap. These tokens empower the community by allowing them to participate in the decision-making process of the platform.
- Rewards and Incentives: Many platforms use fungible tokens as a mechanism to incentivize behaviors or actions. For instance, liquidity providers might earn tokens for staking assets in a decentralized exchange.
- Token Sales & ICOs: Many startups and projects raise capital by issuing fungible tokens to investors. These tokens can represent a myriad of potential utilities within the respective project's ecosystem.

In sum, the flexibility and interchangeability of fungible tokens have made them an integral tool for various applications in the rapidly evolving world of blockchain and cryptocurrencies.

Notes: _____

_____

_____

# Crypto Bites: Snack-sized Insights for the Modern Investor

NFTs in the Digital Art and Entertainment World

Non-Fungible Tokens (NFTs) have emerged as transformative tools in the digital art and entertainment realm. Unlike fungible tokens, which are identical and interchangeable, NFTs are unique and verifiable, ensuring the authenticity of digital assets.

1. Digital Art Authenticity: NFTs have revolutionized the digital art market by providing a blockchain-based proof of ownership and provenance. Artists can mint their artworks as NFTs, ensuring buyers are purchasing authentic and original pieces. The blockchain records every transaction, preventing forgery and allowing buyers and collectors to trace the artwork's ownership history.
2. Monetization for Creators: Traditional digital art could be easily copied and shared, limiting monetization opportunities for artists. NFTs enable artists to sell their works directly to enthusiasts and even earn royalties from future resales, offering a new revenue stream.
3. Entertainment and Collectibles: Beyond art, NFTs have permeated the entertainment industry, from music to film. Musicians release albums as NFTs, and filmmakers tokenize film scenes. The gaming sector, too, has embraced NFTs for in-game items, ensuring their uniqueness and tradeability.

In essence, NFTs in the digital art and entertainment world offer a blend of authenticity, direct monetization, and enhanced user engagement, paving the way for a new creative economy.

Notes: _____

_____

_____

# Crypto Bites: Snack-sized Insights for the Modern Investor

Beyond ERC-20 and ERC-721: Introduction to ERC-1155

The Ethereum ecosystem, known for its vibrant development community, constantly innovates with new token standards. Enter ERC-1155, an evolution in token standards that merges the benefits of its predecessors, ERC-20 and ERC-721.

1. Multi-Token Standard: Unlike ERC-20 (fungible) and ERC-721 (non-fungible), ERC-1155 allows for the creation and management of both token types within a single smart contract. This means that items like game skins, collectibles, and in-game gold can coexist in one contract.
2. Efficiency: Bundling multiple tokens into a single contract reduces the clutter on the Ethereum blockchain. This makes operations more gas-efficient, especially when dealing with bulk transactions.
3. Interoperability: Items minted using ERC-1155 can easily interact with other contracts, enabling functionalities like trading, loaning, or bundling. This makes it an attractive choice for projects seeking to ensure their tokens work fluidly across various platforms and services.
4. Advanced Features: ERC-1155 also supports more complex features like batch transfers, which further optimize multiple token transfers in one transaction.

In essence, ERC-1155 provides a dynamic, efficient, and adaptable standard for projects looking to harness the advantages of both fungible and non-fungible tokens, making it especially useful for sectors like gaming and collectibles.

Notes: _____

_____

_____

Chapter 4: Stablecoins and CBDCs (Central Bank Digital Currencies)

## Stablecoins Explained

In the turbulent world of cryptocurrencies, stablecoins emerge as a calming force, aiming to offer price stability. As the name suggests, stablecoins are cryptocurrencies designed to have a stable value, typically pegged to a reserve like a specific amount of a commodity or fiat currency such as the US dollar.

1. Purpose in the Crypto Ecosystem: Stablecoins play a crucial role in the cryptocurrency domain. They provide a bridge between the traditional fiat system and the decentralized world of cryptocurrencies. Given the often volatile nature of cryptocurrencies like Bitcoin and Ethereum, stablecoins offer users a reprieve from wild price swings, making them particularly useful for traders and those looking to transfer value across the blockchain without significant exposure to price fluctuations.

2. Types of Stablecoins:
    - Collateral-Backed Stablecoins: These are backed one-for-one by reserve assets like the US dollar. For every stablecoin issued, there's an equivalent amount of currency or commodity held in a reserve. Popular examples include USDC and USDT (Tether), where each token corresponds to one US dollar held in a bank account.
    - Crypto-Collateralized Stablecoins: These are over-collateralized by other cryptocurrencies, typically Ethereum. DAI is a primary example where its stability is maintained through mechanisms and smart contracts on the Ethereum blockchain. If the backing crypto's price drops, the system can liquidate assets to keep the stablecoin's value consistent.
    - Algorithmic Stablecoins: Not backed by collateral, these stablecoins maintain their value through algorithms and smart contracts that automatically increase or decrease the supply of the stablecoin in response to price fluctuations.

3. Use Cases: Beyond being a volatility hedge, stablecoins are crucial in decentralized finance (DeFi) protocols for lending, borrowing, and yield farming. They also facilitate smoother crypto-to-crypto trades on exchanges without converting back to traditional fiat, speeding up transactions and reducing costs.

In conclusion, stablecoins, with their inherent stability mechanisms, act as an essential linchpin, bridging the gap between traditional financial systems and the rapidly evolving world of cryptocurrencies.

# Crypto Bites: Snack-sized Insights for the Modern Investor

CBDCs - The Rise of Digital National Currencies

Central Bank Digital Currencies (CBDCs) represent a significant evolution in the monetary landscape, heralding the digitalization of national currencies. Unlike cryptocurrencies which are decentralized and operate outside the traditional financial system, CBDCs are digital versions of a country's national currency, issued and governed by its central bank.

1. Motivations Behind CBDCs:
   - Fostering Financial Inclusion: In many parts of the world, a significant portion of the population remains unbanked or underbanked. CBDCs have the potential to provide these individuals with access to the formal financial system, allowing them to participate more fully in the national economy.
   - Modernizing Payment Infrastructures: The current financial system, with its layers of intermediaries and outdated infrastructure, can be slow and costly. CBDCs offer the promise of real-time, cost-effective transactions, modernizing payment systems to meet the demands of a digital era.
   - Countering Private Stablecoins: The rise of private stablecoins, like USDT and USDC, has caught the attention of many central banks. Concerned about the potential risks associated with these private digital assets, some governments are exploring CBDCs as a way to maintain monetary sovereignty and ensure financial stability.
   - Enhancing Monetary Policy: CBDCs can provide central banks with additional tools for implementing monetary policy, potentially allowing for more precise and efficient interventions in the economy.
2. Implications for the Traditional Financial System: CBDCs represent a paradigm shift, with the potential to reshape the global financial architecture. By offering a state-backed digital currency, they could reduce the role of intermediaries, streamline cross-border transactions, and introduce new monetary tools. However, they also raise concerns about privacy, security, and the potential displacement of commercial banks.

In essence, while CBDCs come with numerous advantages, they also present challenges that need addressing. As they evolve, the interplay between CBDCs, traditional banking, and decentralized cryptocurrencies will be pivotal in shaping the future of global finance.

Notes: _____

_____

_____

## Stablecoin Controversies and Concerns

Stablecoins, despite their beneficial role in providing a bridge between the traditional financial system and the crypto world, have been mired in several controversies and concerns. These digital assets, which are designed to maintain a stable value by being pegged to traditional currencies or other assets, have been under the microscope for various reasons.

1. Regulatory Scrutiny on Tether (USDT):
    o Reserve Claims: One of the most prominent controversies in the stablecoin realm revolves around Tether. Although USDT claims to be backed 1:1 by the US dollar, skeptics have raised concerns about the veracity of these claims. Regulatory bodies have questioned Tether Ltd. regarding its reserve holdings and the actual backing for each USDT token.
    o Transparency Issues: Over the years, there have been calls for more transparency in the way Tether handles its reserves. While Tether has provided some audits and attestations, critics argue that these are not sufficient to prove the complete backing of its circulating supply.
2. Centralization Concerns:
    o Unlike decentralized cryptocurrencies like Bitcoin, many stablecoins are issued and governed by centralized entities. This centralization raises concerns about potential manipulation, censorship, and the possibility of freezes on user funds.
3. Systemic Risks:
    o As stablecoins gain prominence, there's a growing concern about the systemic risks they might introduce. If a major stablecoin were to lose its peg or face a loss of confidence, it could result in significant financial disruptions, not only in the crypto space but also in the broader financial system.
4. Regulatory Challenges:
    o The rise of stablecoins has caught the attention of regulators worldwide. There are concerns that these digital assets could bypass traditional financial regulatory frameworks, leading to potential issues related to money laundering, tax evasion, and even monetary policy disruption.

In conclusion, while stablecoins offer numerous advantages in terms of providing stability in the often volatile crypto market, they are not without their challenges. Ensuring transparency, proper regulatory oversight, and maintaining trust will be crucial for their continued growth and acceptance.

## Comparison: Stablecoins vs. CBDCs

Stablecoins and Central Bank Digital Currencies (CBDCs) are both forms of digital currency that aim to maintain price stability. However, their origins, governance, and potential impact on the global financial system differ significantly.

1. Origins & Governance:
   o Stablecoins are typically issued by private entities and can be backed by a variety of assets such as fiat currencies, other cryptocurrencies, or even algorithms. Popular examples include USDT, USDC, and DAI.
   o CBDCs are digital versions of a country's national currency and are issued and regulated by the central bank of that country. Examples under research or pilot include China's Digital Yuan and the European Central Bank's Digital Euro.
2. Pros & Cons:
   o Stablecoins:
      ▪ *Pros*: Quick to deploy; serves unbanked populations; bridges traditional finance with decentralized systems.
      ▪ *Cons*: Regulatory concerns; potential centralization; transparency issues regarding reserves.
   o CBDCs:
      ▪ *Pros*: Promotes financial inclusion; modernizes payment infrastructure; can counteract private stablecoins' dominance.
      ▪ *Cons*: Concerns about financial surveillance; might stifle private sector innovation; risks of bank disintermediation.
3. Use Cases & Cross-border Payments:
   o Stablecoins enable smooth crypto-to-crypto trades, offer a hedge against crypto volatility, and facilitate quicker cross-border transactions.
   o CBDCs can revolutionize cross-border trade by making transactions more seamless and less costly. However, their potential is dependent on intergovernmental cooperation and compatible technological infrastructures.
4. Future Evolution of Global Financial Systems:
   o Stablecoins, due to their decentralized nature, can propel the global adoption of DeFi platforms and services. Their success, though, hinges on navigating regulatory landscapes.
   o CBDCs represent an evolutionary step in national currencies. They can usher in a new era of digital financial systems where central banks play a direct role in the consumer financial landscape, potentially reshaping banking structures.

In conclusion, while stablecoins and CBDCs both offer stable digital currency options, their differing governance and intended purposes position them uniquely in the evolving digital finance landscape.

Chapter 5: NFTs (Non-Fungible Tokens)

NFT Basics and Token Standards

In the expansive universe of digital assets, a critical distinction lies between two unique types of tokens based on their nature and use cases: NFTs (Non-Fungible Tokens) and traditional cryptographic tokens. This division is paramount not only for comprehending the token's functionality but also for grasping its position in the broader digital economy.

1. Traditional Cryptographic Tokens: These tokens, whether fungible or not, often serve as a medium of exchange, store of value, or unit of account within a specific blockchain ecosystem. Their uniformity ensures interchangeability, where each token holds the same value as another of its kind.

   *Example:* Bitcoin (BTC) is a traditional cryptographic token where every BTC is identical to another and holds the same value. *Unique Characteristics:* Uniformity, divisibility, and broad acceptance characterize these tokens. They function like digital gold or currency within their respective networks.

2. NFTs (Non-Fungible Tokens): NFTs stand out due to their distinctness and indivisibility. Each NFT, governed by standards like ERC-721 or ERC-1155, carries unique metadata or attributes, making it distinct from any other token.

   *Example:* A digital artwork tokenized on the Ethereum blockchain where the token represents ownership of that specific piece of art. *Unique Characteristics:* NFTs redefine digital ownership, authenticity, and provenance. Their distinct nature ensures that no two NFTs are alike, even within the same collection. This uniqueness is rooted in the blockchain, ensuring verifiable rarity and originality.

Conclusion: While traditional cryptographic tokens and NFTs both find their grounding in blockchain technology, they serve divergent purposes. The former acts as digital currency or assets, ensuring seamless transactions and value storage. In contrast, NFTs revolutionize the concept of digital ownership, catering to sectors like art, collectibles, and even intellectual property. Recognizing these differences is crucial for enthusiasts, creators, and investors navigating the dynamic world of digital assets.

Notes: _____

_____

_____

## NFT Use Cases Beyond Art

NFTs, or Non-Fungible Tokens, have garnered significant attention for revolutionizing the world of digital art. However, their utility extends far beyond this domain. The unique nature of NFTs - each token is distinct and verifiable on a blockchain - makes them suitable for a variety of applications:

- Collectibles: Similar to physical collectibles (like baseball cards), NFTs have carved a digital niche. CryptoKitties, for instance, allows users to collect, breed, and sell virtual cats, each having a unique digital DNA.
- Gaming: The gaming industry has seamlessly integrated NFTs. Games like Decentraland and Axie Infinity incorporate NFTs as in-game items, be it land parcels or characters. Players can trade these items, often resulting in real-world profits.
- Music: NFTs are transforming the music industry by allowing artists to sell their work directly to fans. This could be in the form of limited edition tracks, album art, or interactive experiences. It not only provides an additional revenue stream but also strengthens fan-artist interactions.
- Domain Names: Blockchain-based domain names, represented as NFTs, are becoming popular. Platforms like Unstoppable Domains allow users to purchase '.crypto' domains, facilitating decentralized websites and crypto payment addresses.
- Virtual Real Estate: Virtual worlds such as Somnium Space and Cryptovoxels enable users to buy, develop, and sell parcels of land as NFTs. This real estate often hosts virtual events, galleries, or businesses.
- Intellectual Property: Innovators are exploring NFTs for patenting ideas, where tokens represent ownership of a particular innovation. This could streamline the patenting process and create new monetization avenues.

In essence, while art remains a significant segment of the NFT world, the potential applications of NFTs are vast and continuously expanding. As the technology matures, we'll likely witness even more innovative use cases emerging.

Notes: _____

_____

_____

NFT Marketplaces and Platforms

The NFT ecosystem has seen a proliferation of marketplaces and platforms that cater to diverse needs of artists, collectors, and traders. Among these, platforms like OpenSea, Rarible, and NBA Top Shot have emerged as notable players.

- OpenSea: As one of the most comprehensive and popular NFT marketplaces, OpenSea provides a platform for a wide range of digital assets from art and domain names to virtual worlds and collectibles. Its user-friendly interface allows both artists and collectors to easily mint, list, and trade NFTs. OpenSea operates on the Ethereum blockchain and offers a gas-free listing feature. However, a gas fee applies when minting a new item or conducting a sale. OpenSea's approach to copyright verification is reliant on user reporting, meaning that counterfeit or unauthorized content can exist, but community members can report suspicious listings.
- Rarible: Rarible is both a marketplace and a platform that allows users to mint NFTs without coding knowledge. Notably, it introduced the $RARI token, granting governance powers to its community. This decentralized approach allows users to have a say in platform developments. Like OpenSea, Rarible is also on the Ethereum blockchain and has fees associated with transactions. The platform does perform some basic copyright checks, but the onus largely falls on the community to identify and report infringements.
- NBA Top Shot: A licensed collaboration between the NBA and Dapper Labs, NBA Top Shot offers collectible highlights as NFTs. Unlike the former platforms, Top Shot operates on the Flow blockchain, making it more scalable and environmentally efficient. Being officially partnered with the NBA ensures that copyright isn't an issue, as clips are sourced directly from NBA games.

In summary, while these platforms provide a space for NFT transactions, they differ in terms of features, fees, target audience, and approach to copyright verification. As the NFT realm expands, these platforms will likely evolve, and new ones will emerge, each addressing unique market needs.

Notes: _____

_____

_____

# Crypto Bites: Snack-sized Insights for the Modern Investor

Environmental Concerns and NFTs

The meteoric rise of NFTs, particularly those built on the Ethereum blockchain, has been paralleled by a surge in environmental concerns. The crux of these concerns centers on the energy consumption associated with Ethereum's consensus algorithm, Proof of Work (PoW), which requires substantial computational power and thus energy. Since NFT transactions involve Ethereum, each NFT minted, bought, or sold contributes to this energy use, and by extension, to carbon emissions.

Critics point out that the carbon footprint of a single Ethereum transaction can be equivalent to an average household's daily energy consumption. With the popularity of NFTs leading to numerous transactions daily, the cumulative environmental impact is significant. In response, some artists and potential buyers have been deterred from participating in the NFT space, fearing the exacerbation of global environmental issues.

Solutions to mitigate these environmental concerns are in active exploration and development. One such remedy is Ethereum's planned transition from PoW to Proof of Stake (PoS) with its Ethereum 2.0 upgrade. PoS is inherently less energy-intensive, as it replaces miners with validators, reducing the computational power required.

Layer-2 scaling solutions, like Optimistic Rollups and zk-Rollups, which process transactions off the main Ethereum chain, can also lower the environmental impact by reducing the energy required per transaction. Additionally, other eco-friendlier blockchains, like Flow or Tezos, which employ more energy-efficient consensus algorithms, are gaining traction as alternative platforms for minting NFTs.

In conclusion, while the environmental criticisms of NFTs are valid, a combination of technological advancements and a shift in platform preferences may offer a more sustainable path forward for the NFT ecosystem.

Notes: _____

_____

_____

Intellectual Property, Rights, and NFTs

NFTs, or Non-Fungible Tokens, have emerged as a groundbreaking medium to tokenize digital assets, from artwork to music clips. Their decentralized nature, built on blockchain technology, ensures each NFT's uniqueness and provenance. However, the intersection of NFTs and intellectual property rights remains a gray area, sparking significant debate and legal considerations.

At the heart of the discussion is a crucial distinction: owning an NFT does not equate to owning the intellectual property rights of the underlying asset. For instance, purchasing an NFT of a digital painting might give the buyer possession of a unique digital token linked to that artwork. Still, it does not necessarily confer copyright, reproduction rights, or other IP rights related to the artwork itself. This remains true unless explicitly stated in the terms of the NFT sale.

Several controversies have arisen due to this ambiguity. Artists have found their works tokenized as NFTs without permission, leading to potential copyright infringements. Conversely, NFT buyers, under the misconception that they've obtained broader rights, have faced legal consequences when trying to reproduce or commercialize their acquired digital assets.

For artists and creators, it's imperative to understand and clearly specify the rights they are granting (or retaining) when minting NFTs. For buyers, thorough due diligence is essential to ascertain what rights come with an NFT purchase. As the NFT space evolves, clearer guidelines and best practices are emerging, but the onus remains on both creators and consumers to navigate this complex landscape carefully.

Notes: _____

_____

_____

Chapter 6: Wallets and Storage

Understanding Digital Wallets

Cryptocurrency wallets, often termed as digital wallets, are essential tools in the crypto ecosystem. Their primary function isn't just to "store" cryptocurrencies—as coins or tokens aren't stored in a physical sense—but to manage and safeguard the cryptographic keys associated with them.

Key Components:

- Public Key: This is your digital address, somewhat akin to an email address. If someone wants to send you cryptocurrency, they send it to your public key. It's derived from the private key through a cryptographic algorithm and can be shared openly.
- Private Key: Analogous to a password to an email account, this is a secret key that allows you to access and control your funds. Possession of the private key is what grants ownership of the cryptocurrencies associated with a given public key.

Types of Wallets:

1. Software Wallets: These are applications or software-based platforms to manage your crypto keys. They can be:
    - Desktop: Installed on personal computers.
    - Mobile: Smartphone apps.
    - Web: Accessible via browser interfaces.
2. Hardware Wallets: Physical devices, often resembling USB sticks, designed to securely store private keys offline, safeguarding them from online hacking attempts.
3. Paper Wallets: Physical documents containing printed public and private keys. They represent a way of "cold storage"—completely offline.

Interacting with Blockchains:

When you want to send crypto, the wallet software initiates a transaction, signs it with the private key, and broadcasts it to the network. When you receive, the public ledger (blockchain) updates with the new transaction, and the wallet monitors these updates to reflect your current balance.

Digital wallets are more than just storage; they are the management tools for your cryptocurrency assets. Responsible management is crucial to safeguard your digital wealth and enable smooth transactions on the blockchain.

Software Wallets: Desktop, Mobile, and Web-Based Solutions

Software wallets, pivotal in the crypto ecosystem, offer users a digital means to manage and safeguard their cryptographic keys. Depending on their design and platform, these wallets vary in accessibility, user interface, and security features. Here's a deep dive into the primary types: desktop, mobile, and web-based wallets.

1. Desktop Wallets:
   - Accessibility: Installed and run from personal computers, they provide access to your funds from the machine they're installed on.
   - User Interface: Generally comprehensive, offering advanced features for experienced users, such as custom transaction fees or detailed transaction history.
   - Security: While safer than web wallets, they're susceptible to malware or hacks if the computer is compromised. Regular backups are essential.
2. Mobile Wallets:
   - Accessibility: Smartphone apps ensure portability, allowing users to transact on-the-go, often integrating with QR code scanning for convenience.
   - User Interface: Optimized for smaller screens, interfaces are typically user-friendly and streamlined, focusing on essential features.
   - Security: While practical, they can be vulnerable to phone-specific malware or risks like theft or loss. Features like biometric access or two-factor authentication (2FA) enhance security.
3. Web Wallets:
   - Accessibility: Accessible from any device with a web browser, offering high convenience, especially for users who switch devices frequently.
   - User Interface: Varies from simplistic to complex, with some offering exchange integrations for easy trading.
   - Security: Being online, they are exposed to risks like phishing attacks

Notes: _____

_____

_____

# Crypto Bites: Snack-sized Insights for the Modern Investor

Hardware Wallets: Security First

Amid the diverse types of cryptocurrency wallets, hardware wallets stand out due to their unparalleled security features. Serving as dedicated physical devices, these wallets ensure the safekeeping of private keys by keeping them completely offline, thus insulating them from online threats like hacks or malware.

1. The Basics:
   o Offline Security: Unlike software wallets that store keys on internet-connected devices, hardware wallets are inherently cold storage, meaning they're never exposed to the internet unless required.
   o Private Key Isolation: Transactions are signed within the device, ensuring the private key never leaves it, preventing exposure even during transactions.
2. Popular Brands:
   o Ledger: One of the pioneering brands in the hardware wallet space, the Ledger Nano S and Nano X are its flagship products. They come equipped with a secure chip that thwarts attempts to extract keys and supports a wide array of cryptocurrencies.
   o Trezor: Another front-runner, Trezor offers models like Trezor One and Trezor Model T. It's lauded for its open-source software, ensuring transparency and robust community vetting.
3. Benefits:
   o Protection from Online Threats: Immune to viruses and malware, as they never interact directly with potentially compromised systems.
   o Physical Security: Many models feature tamper-evident seals and secure chips, ensuring protection against physical tampering.
   o Backup & Recovery: Typically, upon setup, users are given a mnemonic seed phrase, enabling easy recovery of funds in case the device is lost or damaged.

While hardware wallets entail an upfront cost, the security they offer, especially for substantial amounts of cryptocurrency, justifies the investment. As a best practice, combining them with other wallet types, like using a hardware wallet for savings and a mobile wallet for daily spending, can provide a balance between security and convenience.

Notes: _____

_____

_____

# Crypto Bites: Snack-sized Insights for the Modern Investor

Cold Storage vs. Hot Storage

In the realm of cryptocurrency security, the terms "cold storage" and "hot storage" play pivotal roles, signifying the online or offline status of private keys — the critical components for accessing digital assets. Understanding their differences and applications is essential for safeguarding crypto holdings.

1. Definitions:
   - Cold Storage (Offline): This method involves storing private keys completely offline, ensuring that they're not exposed to the internet. Examples include paper wallets, where private keys are printed or written down, and hardware wallets, where keys are stored on a physical device.
   - Hot Storage (Online): This refers to storing private keys on devices or platforms that are connected to the internet, such as software wallets, exchange accounts, or cloud services.
2. Security Implications:
   - Cold Storage: Being offline, cold storage is immune to online threats like hacking, malware, and phishing. However, it's susceptible to physical threats, such as theft or damage.
   - Hot Storage: While it offers quicker access and convenience, hot storage is vulnerable to online attacks, breaches, and potential platform failures.
3. Best Use Scenarios:
   - Cold Storage: Ideal for long-term storage or "hodling". If you have substantial amounts of crypto you don't plan to access frequently, cold storage is the recommended approach.
   - Hot Storage: Suited for daily transactions and trading. It's best used for funds that you need quick and regular access to.
4. Diversification for Security:
   - Spreading assets across both cold and hot storage can mitigate risks. For instance, one could store the bulk of their holdings in cold storage while keeping a smaller, working amount in hot storage for immediate needs.

In essence, the choice between cold and hot storage hinges on individual needs and preferences. However, adopting a diversified approach ensures a balance between security and convenience, maximizing asset safety.

Notes: _____

_____

_____

# Crypto Bites: Snack-sized Insights for the Modern Investor

Seed Phrases and Wallet Recovery

Seed phrases, often also referred to as mnemonic phrases, are crucial elements in the cryptocurrency ecosystem, serving as lifelines for digital asset ownership. These phrases, typically consisting of 12 to 24 words in a specific order, act as a key to restore and access digital wallets.

1. Purpose of Seed Phrases:
   o Recovery Tool: The primary function of a seed phrase is to act as a recovery mechanism. If a user loses access to their cryptocurrency wallet — be it through hardware failure, loss of a device, or any other reason — the seed phrase allows them to restore their wallet and regain access to their funds on another device or platform.
   o Universal Compatibility: Seed phrases are typically standardized (using the BIP39 standard, for instance), ensuring that they can be used across different wallet software and services.
2. Safety Imperatives:
   o Offline Storage: It's paramount to store seed phrases offline, away from internet-connected devices. Common methods include writing them on paper or engraving them on metal plates to prevent degradation over time.
   o Avoid Digital Copies: Storing seed phrases on cloud services, emails, or taking digital photos can expose them to hacking risks.
   o Physical Safety: Like any valuable item, seed phrases should be kept in secure locations, such as safes, to prevent theft or unintended discovery.
3. Associated Risks:
   o Loss: If you lose your seed phrase and cannot access your wallet, your funds are effectively lost. Unlike traditional banking systems, there's no "forgot password" option.
   o Exposure: If someone else gets access to your seed phrase, they gain full control over your wallet and its contents.

In conclusion, seed phrases are both powerful and delicate tools in the crypto domain. Their diligent management is the cornerstone of digital asset security, emphasizing the age-old adage: "Not your keys, not your coins."

Notes: _____

_____

_____

Chapter 7: Crypto Exchanges

Centralized Exchanges (CEX) Explained

In the bustling cryptocurrency landscape, centralized exchanges (CEXs) play a pivotal role. As hubs of crypto trading and transactions, CEXs have become the mainstream gateway for both novice and seasoned investors alike. But what exactly are they, and how do they operate?

1. The Operational Model: At their core, centralized exchanges are online platforms that function as intermediaries, facilitating the trading of cryptocurrencies for users. Unlike traditional decentralized platforms, CEXs are managed by centralized organizations or entities, making them akin to traditional financial institutions.

2. Notable Players: Several centralized exchanges have risen to prominence due to their robust platforms, security measures, and vast trading volumes. Binance, for instance, is recognized for its vast array of trading pairs and sophisticated trading tools. Coinbase, on the other hand, is lauded for its user-friendly interface, making it an ideal starting point for crypto beginners. Kraken, another notable CEX, is esteemed for its security features and comprehensive regulatory compliance.

3. Custody of Funds: One defining feature of CEXs is the custody of funds. When users deposit funds into a CEX, they essentially entrust the platform with the safekeeping of their assets. In exchange, the user receives an IOU. This means that while users can trade with agility on the platform, they don't hold the private keys to their funds – the exchange does.

4. Intermediary Role: Being intermediaries, CEXs simplify the trading process. Users can easily place buy or sell orders, and the exchange handles order matching, ensuring liquidity. Furthermore, CEXs often provide fiat-to-crypto and vice-versa conversion, bridging the gap between traditional finance and the crypto world.

In summary, while centralized exchanges have facilitated mass adoption of cryptocurrencies, users should be aware of the inherent risks, especially pertaining to fund custody. It's the age-old adage: convenience often comes at the cost of control.

Notes: _____

_____

_____

# Crypto Bites: Snack-sized Insights for the Modern Investor

Decentralized Exchanges (DEX) - A Paradigm Shift

The rise of Decentralized Exchanges (DEXs) has marked a significant shift in the way individuals trade and interact with cryptocurrencies.

1. How DEXs Operate: Unlike their centralized counterparts, DEXs don't rely on a middleman to facilitate trades. Instead, platforms such as Uniswap, SushiSwap, and Kyber Network utilize smart contracts on blockchain networks (primarily Ethereum) to automate the trading process. These contracts allow for direct peer-to-peer exchanges of crypto assets.

2. Leading Platforms:

- Uniswap: Pioneering the Automated Market Maker (AMM) model, Uniswap allows liquidity providers to deposit tokens into pools. Traders then trade against these pools, with a formula determining prices. This model has eliminated the need for order books, often seen in traditional exchanges.
- SushiSwap: Initially a fork of Uniswap, SushiSwap has since differentiated itself by offering new features and a focus on community governance.
- Kyber Network: This platform stands out by aggregating liquidity from various sources, ensuring that users receive competitive rates when they trade.

3. Custody in DEXs: One of the most significant advantages of DEXs is that users retain custody of their assets. Instead of transferring assets to an exchange's wallet, users connect their personal crypto wallets (like MetaMask) directly to the DEX. This direct connection reduces the risk of major exchange hacks, a concern with centralized platforms.

4. DEXs vs. CEXs: Though DEXs offer enhanced control and security, they come with challenges. DEX interfaces can be less user-friendly than centralized ones, and there might be concerns about lower liquidity or higher fees at times. On the other hand, centralized exchanges, with their more traditional infrastructure, can offer higher trading volumes and a perceived ease of use but at the expense of full user control.

In essence, DEXs represent a radical reimagining of exchanges, putting more power in the hands of users while emphasizing transparency and decentralization. However, like all innovations, they come with a set of trade-offs that users must navigate.

Notes: _____

_____

_____

# Crypto Bites: Snack-sized Insights for the Modern Investor

Trading Mechanics and Order Types

Trading in cryptocurrency, like traditional financial markets, involves various order types that determine how trades are executed. Understanding these orders is vital for crafting a coherent trading strategy.

1. Market Orders: A market order is the most straightforward type of order. It allows traders to buy or sell a cryptocurrency at the best available price in the market. Due to its immediacy, market orders are executed quickly, but traders might not always get the exact price they see at the time of placing the order, especially in volatile conditions.

2. Limit Orders: Limit orders enable traders to set a specific price at which they wish to buy or sell. For instance, if Bitcoin is trading at $50,000, a trader can set a limit order to buy it at $48,000. The order will only execute when (or if) the asset reaches that predetermined price. This type of order provides more control over the price but does not guarantee execution.

3. Stop Orders: Stop orders, also known as stop-loss orders, are a protective mechanism. A trader can set a predetermined price at which a coin will be sold, usually to mitigate potential losses. For instance, if Bitcoin is owned at $50,000, setting a stop order at $48,000 will automatically sell the Bitcoin if the price drops to that level.

Centralized vs. Decentralized Exchanges:

- Centralized Exchanges (CEXs): These platforms generally offer a wide range of order types, similar to traditional stock exchanges. Advanced trading interfaces in CEXs allow traders to utilize these orders effectively, benefiting from the platform's liquidity and order matching algorithms.
- Decentralized Exchanges (DEXs): The order mechanisms in DEXs can vary. While some advanced DEXs might offer various order types, many operate using a liquidity pool model without a traditional order book. For instance, Automated Market Makers (AMMs) like Uniswap don't use standard orders but rather swap assets based on preset algorithms.

In summary, the choice of order type can greatly influence trading outcomes, dictating the price, timing, and likelihood of order execution. When trading, it's crucial to comprehend each order type's nuances and the specific environment of the exchange being used.

Notes: _____

_____

_____

# Crypto Bites: Snack-sized Insights for the Modern Investor

Fee Structures - Understanding Costs

Trading on cryptocurrency exchanges isn't free; various fees are charged, shaping a trader's net returns. Here's a deep dive into the most prevalent fee structures and how users can optimize costs:

1. Maker and Taker Fees: These are the most common fees encountered on exchanges. When you place an order that doesn't fill immediately, adding liquidity to the order book, you're a "maker". Conversely, if your order matches an existing one, removing liquidity, you're a "taker".

- Maker Fee: Usually lower than taker fees, this rewards users for providing liquidity.
- Taker Fee: Generally higher, since takers take away liquidity.

2. Withdrawal Fees: Exchanges usually charge a fee when users withdraw assets to a personal wallet. This is often to cover the network transaction cost, but some platforms mark this up for additional revenue.

3. Deposit Fees: Less common, but some exchanges charge a fee for depositing certain assets. This can vary depending on the cryptocurrency.

4. Fee Reduction & Loyalty Programs: Many exchanges, especially centralized ones, offer native tokens (e.g., Binance's BNB or Huobi's HT) which, when held or used for transactions, can grant users significant fee reductions. Additionally, loyalty programs can offer tiered structures where higher trading volumes result in lower fees.

5. Other Costs: There can be hidden costs:

- Slippage: On DEXs, the difference between the expected price of a trade and the executed price can be significant.
- Gas Fees: Especially on Ethereum-based DEXs, users pay for smart contract interactions.

Conclusion: Understanding fee structures is pivotal for traders to maximize profits. While fees may seem small initially, they accumulate over numerous trades. Hence, traders should stay informed and utilize platforms or tokens that minimize costs without compromising security.

Notes: _____

_____

_____

Security Measures and Best Practices

Cryptocurrency exchanges, as hubs of digital wealth, are prime targets for cyber-attacks. Over the years, notable exchange hacks have underscored the imperative for robust security measures. Here's an exploration of the security landscape and best practices adopted by exchanges and users:

1. Past Hacks and Implications: History is replete with exchange breaches. Notably, the Mt. Gox hack in 2014 saw the loss of 850,000 Bitcoins, shaking the crypto world. These incidents highlighted vulnerabilities in exchange architectures and the dire need for enhanced security measures.

2. Evolution of Exchange Security: In response to threats, exchanges have bolstered their security protocols:

- Cold and Hot Wallets: Exchanges now store the majority of funds in cold wallets (offline) to minimize exposure to online threats. Hot wallets (online) hold only necessary operational funds.
- Multi-Signature Wallets: Require multiple private keys to authorize a transaction, adding a layer of security.

3. User-Centric Security Measures: Beyond exchange protocols, users can adopt several practices to ensure safety:

- Two-Factor Authentication (2FA): A second layer of authentication, like an OTP from an app or SMS, protects against unauthorized access.
- Withdrawal Whitelists: Users can specify trusted withdrawal addresses. This limits fund transfers only to whitelisted addresses, preventing malicious withdrawals.
- Phishing Awareness: Users must be wary of phishing attempts, always verifying website URLs and avoiding suspicious email links.

4. Ongoing Vigilance: Despite enhanced security, the dynamic nature of threats demands continuous upgrades and vigilance. Newer technologies like hardware security modules (HSM) are emerging to fortify exchange defenses.

Conclusion: While exchanges evolve their security postures, users must prioritize personal safety measures. A holistic, layered approach to security ensures that both exchanges and their patrons can safeguard digital assets against an ever-evolving threat landscape.

# Crypto Bites: Snack-sized Insights for the Modern Investor

Chapter 8: Crypto Index Funds and ETFs

Introduction to Crypto Index Funds

The evolution of financial markets is marked by innovations aimed at democratizing access and simplifying investment processes. In the cryptocurrency domain, one such innovation that stands out is the emergence of Crypto Index Funds.

1. What are Crypto Index Funds?:
   o Much like traditional index funds in the stock market, crypto index funds are designed to track a selection of cryptocurrencies. Instead of putting one's capital into a single cryptocurrency, investors can buy into an index fund, which comprises a diversified mix or "basket" of different cryptocurrencies. The exact composition and weighting can vary, typically based on market capitalization or other criteria.
2. Diversified Exposure:
   o The primary advantage of crypto index funds lies in their diversification. The volatile nature of individual cryptocurrencies can present considerable risks. By spreading investments across multiple digital assets, these risks are, to some extent, mitigated. If one cryptocurrency in the basket underperforms, it may be balanced out by others that perform well.
3. Appeal to Passive Investors:
   o Crypto index funds cater to a segment of investors who prefer a more passive investment strategy. Instead of actively trading individual cryptocurrencies and continually adjusting their portfolio, investors can buy into an index fund and achieve automatic diversification. This not only reduces the need for constant market monitoring but also aligns with a long-term investment horizon.
4. Reduced Barriers to Entry:
   o For newcomers to the crypto space, the sheer number of available cryptocurrencies can be overwhelming. Crypto index funds simplify the decision-making process by offering an already curated and diversified portfolio, making it easier for newcomers to gain market exposure.

In conclusion, crypto index funds represent an amalgamation of traditional finance principles with the new-age digital asset realm. By offering diversification and simplifying the investment process, they present an attractive proposition for both seasoned and novice investors venturing into the crypto world.

Notes: _____

_____

_____

Crypto ETFs Explained

The financial landscape has been buzzing with the integration of cryptocurrencies into traditional investment vehicles. Among these innovations, Crypto ETFs (Exchange-Traded Funds) have emerged as a notable intersection between conventional finance and the burgeoning world of digital assets.

1. What are Crypto ETFs?:
   o Akin to traditional ETFs, which track indices, commodities, or a basket of assets, Crypto ETFs are designed to track one or more digital assets, like Bitcoin or Ethereum. Rather than purchasing the actual cryptocurrency, investors buy shares of the ETF, which represent an underlying holding of the cryptocurrency or a portfolio of multiple cryptocurrencies. These ETFs are listed and traded on conventional stock exchanges.
2. Liquidity and Accessibility:
   o Crypto ETFs enhance liquidity by making it possible for investors to get exposure to cryptocurrencies without going through the process of buying, storing, and managing them directly. They can be bought or sold like any other stock, bringing an element of familiarity to those transitioning from traditional finance.
3. Broader Market Adoption:
   o The introduction of crypto ETFs is often viewed as a stamp of legitimacy for the cryptocurrency industry. By providing a regulated and more familiar means of investment, they can attract a wider range of participants, including those who might have been previously hesitant to enter the uncharted waters of direct cryptocurrency investment.
4. Institutional Investment:
   o One of the most significant implications of crypto ETFs is the potential to draw institutional investors. Given their preference for regulated, transparent, and familiar investment vehicles, ETFs offer institutions a more palatable entry point into the crypto domain.
5. Considerations and Implications:
   o While crypto ETFs offer ease and accessibility, they also come with their own set of considerations. The underlying assets are held by a third party, which can introduce counterparty risk. Additionally, fees associated with ETF management can impact returns.

In essence, crypto ETFs represent a bridge between the innovative world of digital assets and the established realm of traditional finance. They play a pivotal role in expanding the reach of cryptocurrencies and facilitating a more inclusive and regulated investment environment.

Advantages and Risks of Crypto Index Funds and ETFs

As the bridge between the traditional finance world and the emerging digital asset space strengthens, Crypto Index Funds and ETFs have become prominent investment vehicles. Here's a concise analysis of their advantages and inherent risks.

Advantages:

1. Diversification: One of the primary benefits of Crypto Index Funds and ETFs is diversification. Instead of betting on a single cryptocurrency, these instruments spread the investment across multiple assets, thereby potentially reducing the risk associated with the volatility of individual coins.
2. Simplicity: For those new to the crypto world, navigating the myriad of coins can be daunting. Crypto Index Funds and ETFs simplify the investment process by offering a curated basket of cryptocurrencies, negating the need for individual selection and research.
3. Reduced Volatility: By virtue of diversification, these instruments can help mitigate the extreme price swings that single cryptocurrencies often experience. Though the crypto market, in general, is volatile, a well-balanced fund might weather the storms more gracefully.

Risks:

1. Management Fees: Just as with traditional index funds and ETFs, their crypto counterparts usually come with management fees. These fees, which pay for the professional management of the fund, can eat into potential profits, especially in comparison to direct investments.
2. Tracking Errors: Ideally, a crypto ETF or index fund should closely track its underlying benchmark or assets. However, discrepancies, called tracking errors, can arise, leading to performance that might diverge from what an investor expects based on the index or basket it's mirroring.
3. Reliance on Fund Managers: While professional management can be an advantage, it's also a double-edged sword. Investors place trust in fund managers to make the right decisions, but those decisions might not always align with individual investment goals or risk tolerance.

In conclusion, while Crypto Index Funds and ETFs offer a more structured and potentially less volatile gateway into the crypto space, they aren't devoid of risks. As with any investment, thorough research, understanding of fee structures, and awareness of potential discrepancies between fund performance and underlying assets are crucial.

# Crypto Bites: Snack-sized Insights for the Modern Investor

Regulatory Landscape and Major Players in Crypto ETFs and Index Funds

The crypto ecosystem has experienced tremendous growth, drawing increased attention from regulatory bodies across the globe. Particularly, the advent of crypto ETFs and index funds has spurred diverse regulatory responses and led to the emergence of notable market players.

Regulatory Landscape:

1. U.S. SEC's Position: Historically, the U.S. Securities and Exchange Commission (SEC) has been cautious about crypto ETFs. Their concerns primarily revolve around market manipulation, fraud, and the liquidity of underlying assets. However, with growing institutional interest and more mature crypto market infrastructure, the SEC's stance has been closely watched for signs of a shift towards approving Bitcoin ETFs.
2. Global Approaches: While the U.S. has been cautious, other jurisdictions have been more welcoming. For instance, Canada approved its first Bitcoin ETF in early 2021, marking a significant milestone. Similarly, several European countries have granted permissions for crypto-based investment products, recognizing the evolving nature of the asset class and aiming to offer investors regulated exposure.

Major Players:

1. Grayscale's Bitcoin Trust (GBTC): Grayscale is a significant player in offering institutional and retail investors exposure to Bitcoin without directly holding the cryptocurrency. GBTC, while not an ETF, functions similarly, with its shares representing a certain amount of Bitcoin.
2. Pioneering ETFs in Canada: Purpose Bitcoin ETF became Canada's first-ever approved Bitcoin ETF, and it marked a watershed moment for crypto investments in North America.
3. European Innovators: In Europe, products like the ETC Group's Bitcoin ETP (exchange-traded product) have paved the way, offering investors a regulated avenue to gain exposure to Bitcoin's price movements.

In conclusion, while regulatory landscapes differ by jurisdiction, there's a clear trend towards more structure and oversight in the crypto ETF and index fund spaces. As regulators grapple with the intricacies of the digital asset world, market players are continuously innovating to offer investors safe and transparent vehicles to access the burgeoning world of cryptocurrencies.

Chapter 9: Decentralized Finance (DeFi)

Foundations of DeFi

Decentralized Finance, commonly known as DeFi, represents a radical shift in the world of finance, challenging traditional structures and intermediaries. Built primarily on blockchain platforms like Ethereum, DeFi offers an innovative ecosystem wherein financial applications, services, and products are open to anyone with an internet connection. Let's delve into its foundational elements:

1. Core Principles:
   o Permissionless: DeFi platforms are open for anyone to access without requiring any permissions. This is in stark contrast to traditional banking systems where one needs to qualify for financial products.
   o Transparency: All transactions and smart contract rules in DeFi are open and verifiable on the blockchain. This transparent nature fosters trust among users.
   o Interoperability: DeFi products are often designed as modular building blocks, known as "money legos," allowing seamless interactions and integrations between them.
2. Democratizing Finance: At its heart, DeFi aims to democratize access to financial services. Whether it's lending, borrowing, trading, or saving, DeFi platforms are accessible irrespective of geographical boundaries or economic status. This opens up opportunities for financial inclusion, especially for the unbanked and underbanked populations.
3. Blockchain as the Foundation: The decentralized nature of blockchains makes them the ideal backbone for DeFi. They provide:
   o Trust: Transactions are immutable and transparent, ensuring integrity.
   o Censorship Resistance: Decentralized networks are robust against regulatory or organizational interference.
   o Smart Contracts: These self-executing contracts automate and control the agreement between parties, serving as the underpinning for many DeFi applications.
4. Replacing Intermediaries: Traditional financial systems often involve various intermediaries, each adding complexity, costs, and potential points of failure. DeFi, by design, minimizes intermediaries, allowing peer-to-peer interactions, reducing costs, and increasing efficiency.

In conclusion, DeFi has ushered in a new paradigm, aiming to revolutionize the financial landscape. By capitalizing on blockchain technology, it promises a more inclusive, efficient, and transparent financial future.

# Crypto Bites: Snack-sized Insights for the Modern Investor

Lending and Borrowing Protocols in DeFi

The DeFi sector has redefined lending and borrowing, offering decentralized platforms where users can lend their assets to earn interest or borrow assets against collateral. Here's a closer look at this burgeoning domain:

1. Basics:
   - Unlike traditional systems that rely on intermediaries like banks, DeFi platforms employ smart contracts on blockchains, allowing peer-to-peer transactions without intermediaries.
   - Users can lend their crypto assets, earning interest as passive income. Conversely, they can borrow by locking up a certain amount of cryptocurrency as collateral.

2. Leading Platforms:
   - MakerDAO: A decentralized credit platform on Ethereum. Users lock up assets (e.g., ETH) as collateral to mint DAI, a stablecoin pegged to the USD. This is often over-collateralized to minimize risk.
   - Compound: Allows users to lend or borrow popular cryptocurrencies. Interest rates are algorithmically adjusted based on supply and demand.

3. Over-Collateralization:
   - To manage the inherent volatility of cryptocurrencies, most DeFi lending platforms require borrowers to provide collateral exceeding the loan's value, often significantly. This acts as a safety buffer, ensuring lenders get repaid even if asset values drop.

4. Managing Volatility and Risk:
   - Liquidation: If the collateral's value drops and crosses a certain threshold, the platform may automatically liquidate a portion to ensure the loan's value is covered. Borrowers are incentivized to monitor and maintain their collateral ratios to avoid this.
   - Stablecoins: Platforms often employ stablecoins like DAI or USDC, which are pegged to stable assets like the USD. This counters crypto's volatility in lending/borrowing scenarios.

5. Incentives:
   - Beyond interest rates, platforms may incentivize participation through governance tokens or other rewards, ensuring a vibrant ecosystem.

In summation, DeFi lending and borrowing offer a revolutionary approach to finance, enabling greater accessibility and flexibility. However, with high rewards come inherent risks, necessitating users to be well-informed and cautious.

# Crypto Bites: Snack-sized Insights for the Modern Investor

Decentralized Exchanges (DEXs) and Automated Market Makers (AMMs)

As cryptocurrency evolves, so does the infrastructure supporting its trade. Two innovations—Decentralized Exchanges (DEXs) and Automated Market Makers (AMMs)—have transformed how users swap assets.

1. Decentralized Exchanges (DEXs):
   o Definition: Unlike traditional centralized exchanges (e.g., Coinbase or Binance) that rely on intermediaries to facilitate trades, DEXs operate without a central authority, enabling peer-to-peer trades directly on the blockchain.
   o Benefits:
     ▪ Security: Since users retain control of their private keys, there's less risk of large-scale hacks that centralized exchanges sometimes suffer.
     ▪ Censorship Resistance: Operating in a decentralized manner, DEXs are less susceptible to regulatory crackdowns or geopolitical pressures.
     ▪ Accessibility: Anyone with an internet connection can access DEXs, ensuring greater inclusivity.
   o Challenges: Historically, DEXs faced issues like lower liquidity and slower trade speeds, but these are being addressed with new technologies like AMMs.
2. Automated Market Makers (AMMs):
   o Definition: AMMs are algorithms that set the price of tokens and facilitate trades in a decentralized manner. Instead of matching buyers with sellers, as traditional order books do, AMMs use liquidity pools to fulfill trade requests.
   o Liquidity Pools: Users can deposit assets into pools, which are then used for trading. In return, they earn fees from the trades.
   o Popular Protocols: Uniswap and PancakeSwap are popular DEXs using the AMM model.
   o Benefits: AMMs address the liquidity challenge faced by early DEXs, often providing competitive rates and faster trades.
   o Risks: "Impermanent Loss" is a potential downside for liquidity providers when the price of provided tokens changes significantly.

In summation, DEXs and AMMs symbolize a shift towards a more decentralized and inclusive financial landscape. While they usher in numerous benefits, users should also be aware of the associated risks and nuances of these platforms. As with all things crypto, a mix of innovation and user diligence is shaping the future.

Yield Farming and Liquidity Mining

ield farming, at its essence, is the act of leveraging different DeFi protocols and platforms to earn returns on one's cryptocurrency holdings, akin to an investor seeking the best interest rate or yield. Here's a brief examination of this concept:

1. Core Concepts:
   o Staking/Locking Assets: In yield farming, users "stake" or lock up their crypto assets in a DeFi platform, typically in a liquidity pool.
   o Liquidity Mining: Beyond just staking, liquidity mining involves providing liquidity to a platform (usually in the form of token pairs) and earning rewards, often in the form of a platform's native token.
2. Potential Returns:
   o The attraction of yield farming is the prospect of high returns, sometimes reaching triple-digit annual percentage yields (APY). These returns arise from a combination of transaction fees, liquidity mining rewards, and sometimes bonus tokens.
3. Strategies:
   o Advanced yield farmers hop between platforms and strategies to maximize returns. They might leverage multiple platforms at once, compound returns by reinvesting earned tokens, or even take on debt to increase their staked amount.
4. Governance Tokens:
   o Many DeFi platforms distribute governance tokens to liquidity providers. These tokens can be a source of additional yield and often grant holders the right to vote on platform updates or changes. A notable example is COMP from Compound.
5. Risks:
   o High returns often come with high risks. Liquidity can be impermanent, resulting in potential losses if asset prices swing dramatically. Smart contract vulnerabilities or platform bugs can also pose significant threats.

In essence, while yield farming offers lucrative opportunities in the DeFi space, participants should be well-informed of the strategies and inherent risks. Proper due diligence and understanding can help navigate this dynamic landscape.

Notes: _____

_____

_____

# Crypto Bites: Snack-sized Insights for the Modern Investor

DeFi Governance and DAOs (Decentralized Autonomous Organizations)

In the realm of DeFi, a fundamental shift away from centralized control is underway, with decision-making processes becoming more democratized. Two pivotal elements in this decentralization are DeFi Governance and DAOs. Here's a closer look:

1. DeFi Governance:
    o Purpose: Governance in DeFi pertains to the decision-making processes regarding the rules, development, and future trajectory of a protocol.
    o Governance Tokens: Most DeFi platforms issue their native governance tokens (e.g., COMP for Compound, MKR for MakerDAO). Holders of these tokens have the right to propose or vote on changes to the protocol. This mechanism allows for community-driven direction rather than a centralized entity making all decisions.
2. Decentralized Autonomous Organizations (DAOs):
    o Definition: DAOs are organizations governed by rules encoded as computer programs on a blockchain. They operate autonomously with members coordinating through smart contracts.
    o Community-Led: Unlike traditional organizations, DAOs lack a centralized leadership. Instead, decisions are reached through consensus mechanisms, often involving token-based voting.
    o Applications in DeFi: Many DeFi projects adopt the DAO model to manage funds, decide on protocol upgrades, or even distribute grants for community development.
3. Impact on DeFi:
    o Resilience and Trust: DAOs and decentralized governance foster trust since decisions are transparent and made collectively. This can potentially make protocols more resilient to external pressures and censorship.
    o Challenges: However, the model is not without challenges. Voter participation can be low, and there's potential for large token holders ("whales") to have disproportionate influence.

In summary, as DeFi continues its trajectory, the evolution and refinement of decentralized governance and DAOs will be pivotal in determining how projects adapt, grow, and serve their communities. This shift represents not just a technological evolution, but a profound change in how organizational decisions can be made in the digital age.

Notes: _____

_____

_____

Chapter 10: Crypto Mining

Basics of Cryptocurrency Mining

Cryptocurrency mining is a foundational element of many decentralized networks, ensuring transaction validity, network security, and enabling the creation of new crypto units.

1. What is Mining?: At its core, mining involves solving complex mathematical problems using computational power. When a problem is solved, a new block is added to the blockchain. This process ensures that transactions are validated and recorded on the blockchain in a chronological and immutable manner.

2. Role in Transaction Validation: Transactions made across a network are grouped into blocks. Miners pick up these blocks and attempt to verify them. To do this, they solve cryptographic puzzles. Once solved, the block is added to the chain, and the transactions within it are considered confirmed. This meticulous process prevents double-spending and ensures the integrity of the network.

3. Creation of New Cryptocurrency Units: A crucial byproduct of the mining process is the 'block reward'. Upon successfully adding a block to the chain, miners are rewarded with freshly minted cryptocurrency. This serves two primary purposes: incentivizing miners to commit resources to the network, and introducing new coins into circulation in a controlled manner.

4. Miners: The Decentralized Auditors: Miners are, in essence, decentralized auditors of the blockchain. They invest computational resources to ensure transactions are genuine and, in return, maintain the security and integrity of the entire network. This decentralized nature prevents any single entity from gaining control or acting maliciously.

In Conclusion: Cryptocurrency mining is more than just the creation of new coins. It's a rigorous validation process that upholds the decentralized, secure, and transparent ideals of blockchain networks. Through their efforts, miners sustain the very heart of what makes cryptocurrencies revolutionary.

Notes: _____

_____

_____

Proof of Work (PoW) vs. Proof of Stake (PoS)

Consensus algorithms lie at the heart of every cryptocurrency, ensuring transactions are recorded correctly and malicious actors are kept at bay. Two of the most prominent algorithms are Proof of Work (PoW) and Proof of Stake (PoS), each with its own merits and challenges.

1. Proof of Work (PoW):

- Functionality: In PoW, miners compete to solve cryptographic puzzles. The first to solve it gets to add a new block to the blockchain, receiving a block reward in return.
- Energy Intensity: The PoW process is resource-intensive. As the puzzles become harder over time (to regulate coin production rate and ensure network security), they require more computational power, leading to increased energy consumption.
- Security: The sheer computational power involved in PoW makes attacks like the 51% attack costly and less feasible, offering a high degree of security to networks.
- Environmental Concerns: The major downside of PoW is its environmental footprint. Large-scale mining farms, especially those relying on non-renewable energy sources, have a significant carbon output.

2. Proof of Stake (PoS):

- Functionality: In PoS, validators are chosen to create new blocks based on the number of coins they hold and are willing to "stake" or lock up as collateral. Essentially, the more you're invested in the network, the higher the chance you'll be chosen to validate a block of transactions.
- Energy Efficiency: PoS is far less energy-intensive than PoW, as it doesn't require massive amounts of computational work.
- Security: PoS also deters malicious actions; attacking the network would devalue the attacker's staked coins.
- Critiques: Some argue PoS may lead to coin concentration, where only the wealthy have a significant say in the network's direction.

In Conclusion: While PoW's security and decentralized nature have proven effective, concerns over its environmental impact have led many newer cryptocurrencies to adopt or consider the PoS model. Both methods have their strengths and weaknesses, and the debate about which is superior continues in the crypto community.

Mining Hardware – ASICs, GPUs, and CPUs

Cryptocurrency mining has seen a dramatic evolution in hardware, paralleling the rise in the crypto industry's complexity and value. The progression can be understood as moving from CPUs to GPUs and, finally, to ASICs, each leap aiming for increased efficiency and power.

1. CPU (Central Processing Unit) Mining:

- Early Days: In the infancy of cryptocurrencies, specifically Bitcoin, miners used CPUs for mining. These are general-purpose processors found in most computers.
- Efficiency: While accessible and easy for enthusiasts to get started, CPUs are not optimized for the kind of repetitive calculations required for mining.
- Decline: As the network grew and the competition among miners intensified, CPU mining became inefficient in terms of profitability and power consumption.

2. GPU (Graphics Processing Unit) Mining:

- Rise: Miners soon moved to GPUs, which are better suited for parallel processing tasks, making them more efficient for the repetitive nature of crypto mining.
- Flexibility: GPUs, found in many gaming computers, can mine multiple cryptocurrencies and aren't limited to one specific task, unlike ASICs.
- Popularity: Their relative affordability and availability led to a boom in GPU mining, with many setting up "mining rigs" using multiple graphics cards.

3. ASIC (Application-Specific Integrated Circuit) Miners:

- Specialization: ASIC miners are custom-built for a specific crypto mining task, making them incredibly efficient at it.
- Performance: Their high hash rate (mining power) means they're more likely to earn the associated crypto rewards, outperforming GPUs in pure performance metrics.
- Controversy: ASICs are expensive and can be cost-prohibitive for casual miners. This has led to concerns about mining centralization, as only those who can afford these specialized machines dominate the mining landscape.
- Network Specificity: They're designed for specific cryptocurrency networks, meaning a Bitcoin ASIC miner isn't suitable for mining Ethereum.

Conclusion: The evolution from CPUs to ASICs mirrors the increasing professionalization and commercialization of crypto mining. While ASICs are dominant in networks like Bitcoin, there are efforts in some crypto communities to resist ASIC dominance, aiming to keep mining decentralized and accessible.

Mining Pools and Their Dynamics

As cryptocurrencies matured, the increasing difficulty of mining meant that individual miners faced dwindling chances of successfully mining a block and receiving rewards. Mining pools emerged as a solution, enabling miners to combine computational resources and increase their collective odds of earning rewards.

1. What are Mining Pools?: Mining pools are collaborative efforts where individual miners contribute their hash power to a centralized pool. The pool, in turn, focuses its combined power on mining blocks. When the pool successfully mines a block, rewards are distributed among participants based on their contributed computational power.

2. Distribution Methods: Different pools have different reward distribution systems, including:

- Pay-Per-Share (PPS): Miners get a set payment for each share of computational power they contribute, regardless of whether the pool mines a block.
- Proportional: Miners receive rewards in proportion to the number of shares they contributed to the pool during a round. A round ends when the pool successfully mines a block.

3. Advantages of Mining Pools:

- Consistent Earnings: Individual miners might go extended periods without mining a block. Pools provide more regular, albeit smaller, earnings.
- Reduced Variance: Combining resources reduces the 'luck' factor, leading to more predictable mining outcomes.

4. Implications on Mining Decentralization:

- Centralization Concerns: Large mining pools can command significant portions of a network's total hash power. If a few pools dominate, it raises concerns about network security and the decentralized ethos of cryptocurrencies.
- Potential for Collusion: Overly centralized mining power could theoretically allow for collusion, where dominant pools might attempt to manipulate the network in malicious ways.

Conclusion: While mining pools offer individual miners more consistent returns, they introduce complexities to the decentralization dynamics of cryptocurrency networks. As with many facets of the crypto ecosystem, there's a balance to be struck between efficiency and maintaining decentralization principles.

Economic Implications of Mining

Cryptocurrency mining, at its core, is the process of validating and recording transactions on a blockchain. However, beyond its technical function, mining has significant economic implications both for individual miners and the broader crypto market. Economic Implications of Mining

1. Costs of Mining:

- Equipment: As the complexity of cryptographic puzzles increases, the need for powerful hardware such as ASICs and GPUs rises. These pieces of hardware are often expensive to purchase and maintain.
- Electricity: Mining consumes vast amounts of electricity. The costs vary based on energy prices in the miner's location, but it's generally a significant expense.
- Operational Costs: This includes cooling, housing, and maintaining mining rigs. In regions with warmer climates, cooling costs can be substantial.

2. Mining Rewards and Profitability: The potential rewards from mining comprise block rewards and transaction fees. Miners weigh these potential earnings against the costs to determine profitability. It's worth noting that as more miners join a network, competition increases, and the probability of earning rewards can decrease.

3. The "Halving" and Its Implications: Periodically, events known as "halvings" occur in certain cryptocurrencies, notably Bitcoin. During a halving, the block rewards given to miners are cut in half.

- Supply Reduction: Halvings effectively reduce the new supply of coins entering the market.
- Price Implications: The reduced supply often leads to speculative theories about potential price increases. Historically, Bitcoin has seen significant price rallies post-halving, though other factors also play a role.
- Miner Behavior: Reduced rewards can squeeze miner profitability. Less efficient miners might exit, potentially leading to mining centralization among well-funded entities.

Conclusion: Mining plays a pivotal role in cryptocurrency networks. Its economic implications ripple through areas like equipment manufacturing, energy consumption patterns, and even the broader crypto market dynamics, especially during significant events like halvings.

Chapter 11: Tokenomics

Introduction to Tokenomics

Tokenomics, a portmanteau of "token" and "economics," refers to the economic model surrounding a cryptocurrency or token. It's a crucial blueprint for any crypto project, dictating how the token operates within its ecosystem. Tokenomics encompasses a myriad of factors that determine the token's value, utility, and long-term viability.

1. Coin Supply: This defines how many tokens will exist. It can be:

- Fixed: A capped maximum supply, like Bitcoin's 21 million.
- Inflationary: Tokens have a perpetual creation rate, which can lead to reduced buying power over time.
- Deflationary: Some tokens employ mechanisms where a portion is burned or destroyed, reducing the supply over time.

2. Distribution Methods: This relates to how tokens are allocated and spread. Common methods include:

- Initial Coin Offerings (ICOs): Tokens are sold to early investors.
- Mining or Staking Rewards: Tokens are earned through network participation.
- Airdrops: Free token distribution to holders of an existing cryptocurrency.

3. Utility: Tokens need a purpose within their ecosystem. Utility can be:

- Currency: Used to transact within and outside the ecosystem.
- Governance: Grants holders voting rights on project decisions.
- Access: Required to use certain functionalities of a platform.

4. Incentives: A balanced tokenomic model ensures stakeholders are motivated to support the ecosystem. Incentives can be staking rewards, governance participation, or fee reductions.

5. Sustainability: For long-term viability, the economic model should consider factors like transaction fees, rewards adjustments, and potential token sinks or burn mechanisms.

Conclusion: Tokenomics is the backbone of a cryptocurrency project, dictating its operational dynamics and value proposition. A robust tokenomic model ensures that the token has intrinsic value, serves a purpose, and fosters a sustainable and growing ecosystem. Proper tokenomics can be the difference between a successful project and one that fades into obscurity.

# Crypto Bites: Snack-sized Insights for the Modern Investor

Utility Tokens vs. Security Tokens

In the vast landscape of cryptocurrencies and tokens, two primary categories emerge based on function and purpose: utility tokens and security tokens. These classifications are not just essential for understanding the token's role but also have significant regulatory implications.

1. Utility Tokens: Utility tokens, as the name suggests, provide users with access to a specific product or service within a project's ecosystem. They are not intended as investments in the traditional sense but are essential for certain functionalities.

- Example: Ethereum's ETH is a utility token used to pay for transaction fees and computational services on the Ethereum network.
- Regulatory Stance: Utility tokens, when designed correctly, often escape stringent regulatory frameworks associated with securities. However, if misrepresented or marketed with the promise of future profits, they can attract regulatory scrutiny.

2. Security Tokens: Security tokens derive their value from an external, tradable asset and represent ownership in that asset. They are akin to traditional securities, with the added benefit of blockchain's transparency and decentralization.

- Example: A token that represents shares in a company or real estate project.
- Regulatory Implications: These tokens are subjected to securities regulations in most jurisdictions. Issuers must adhere to registration requirements, periodic disclosures, and anti-fraud regulations. Holders might also face restrictions on transferability and trading.

Conclusion: While both utility and security tokens play a pivotal role in the crypto ecosystem, they cater to different needs and face distinct regulatory landscapes.

Utility tokens provide access to blockchain-based services, whereas security tokens offer a bridge between traditional finance and the digital world, representing real-world assets on the blockchain. Investors and project creators must be acutely aware of the distinctions to navigate the space compliantly and effectively.

Notes: _____

_____

_____

# Crypto Bites: Snack-sized Insights for the Modern Investor

Token Distribution Mechanisms

Token distribution mechanisms play a crucial role in defining the economic landscape and decentralization of a cryptocurrency project. A project's distribution approach can influence token value, adoption rate, and overall ecosystem health.

1. Initial Coin Offerings (ICOs): An ICO is a fundraising mechanism where new tokens are sold to investors. It gained immense popularity during 2017-2018 but was also infamous for scams and failed projects.

- Impact: ICOs can raise significant capital quickly but have faced scrutiny due to lack of regulation, leading to potential price volatility and investor losses.

2. Security Token Offerings (STOs): STOs are a more regulated version of ICOs, where tokens represent an underlying asset or equity.

- Impact: While STOs offer better protection for investors and clarity for issuers, they might have less public appeal due to regulations and accredited investor requirements.

3. Airdrops: Tokens are distributed for free to holders of an existing cryptocurrency. It's often a promotional activity or part of a network split.

- Impact: Airdrops can boost adoption and awareness. However, sudden influxes of free tokens might lead to short-term sell-offs, affecting the token's value.

4. Staking Rewards: Users lock up their tokens to support network operations like transaction validation and, in return, earn additional tokens.

- Impact: Staking incentivizes users to hold their tokens, potentially stabilizing the token's price, but excessive rewards can lead to inflation.

5. Mining Rewards: In Proof of Work systems, miners receive tokens for validating and recording transactions.

- Impact: Mining ensures network security and decentralization. However, the competitive nature of mining might lead to centralization in mining pools.

Conclusion: Each distribution mechanism has its merits and downsides, influencing token economics, decentralization, and project growth. While some methods foster rapid adoption, others might focus on investor protection or network security. A balanced, transparent approach to token distribution is key for the long-term success of any crypto project.

# Crypto Bites: Snack-sized Insights for the Modern Investor

Token Supply Models

Cryptocurrencies adopt various token supply models to determine the availability and issuance of tokens. These models play pivotal roles in a token's value, its perception of scarcity, and incentives for network users.

1. Fixed Supply:

- Example: Bitcoin has a fixed cap of 21 million coins.
- Implications: Fixed supplies create scarcity, which can drive demand if adoption and use increase. It's often seen as a hedge against traditional inflationary currencies, mirroring assets like gold.

2. Inflationary Model:

- Concept: There's a continuous addition of new tokens to the system at predetermined rates or conditions.
- Implications: Inflation can incentivize certain behaviors, like staking or participating as a validator. However, if not balanced correctly, it might lead to a decrease in token value over time.

3. Deflationary Model:

- Concept: The total token supply decreases over time, often due to mechanisms like token burning.
- Implications: By reducing supply, deflationary models can create perceived value and scarcity. Binance Coin (BNB), for instance, employs token burns to periodically reduce its supply.

4. Hybrid Models:

- Concept: A mix of both inflationary and deflationary elements. For example, a token might have an initial inflationary period followed by a fixed cap.
- Implications: Hybrid models aim to benefit from both inflationary and deflationary aspects, balancing network security incentives with long-term value appreciation.

Conclusion: The choice of a token supply model profoundly impacts a cryptocurrency's economic dynamics. While fixed supply coins might appeal to those wary of traditional inflation, inflationary tokens can better incentivize network participation. Deflationary tokens offer an alternative for value appreciation through reduced supply. Ultimately, the design should align with the project's goals, ensuring sustainability and incentivizing desired behaviors.

# Crypto Bites: Snack-sized Insights for the Modern Investor

Token Burns and Buybacks

Token burns and buybacks are strategies used by crypto projects to manage their token supply, potentially enhance value, and instill confidence among token holders.

1. Token Burns:

- Concept: This involves the deliberate and permanent removal of a certain number of tokens from circulation. This is often done by sending these tokens to a public and inaccessible address, commonly known as a "burn address."
- Implications:
    - Supply Reduction: Decreasing the total number of tokens can introduce scarcity, which, if demand remains constant or increases, can drive up the token's value.
    - Demonstrated Commitment: Token burns can be a signal from the project team about their confidence in the token's future.
    - Utility: Some tokens, like Binance Coin (BNB), integrate burns as part of their use-case. For instance, a portion of tokens used in a transaction might be burned.

2. Token Buybacks:

- Concept: Similar to stock buybacks in traditional finance, a project repurchases its tokens, usually from the open market. These tokens can then either be burned or stored.
- Implications:
    - Price Support: By introducing additional demand, buybacks can exert upward pressure on token prices.
    - Confidence Signal: Much like token burns, buybacks can signal a project's confidence in its token and future prospects.
    - Reinvestment: Instead of using profits for developments or marketing, projects reinvest in their token, benefiting all holders.

Conclusion: Both token burns and buybacks are tools for projects to regulate their token supply, stabilize their token's economics, and potentially enhance value. While effective in the short term, their long-term success relies on the project's fundamentals and genuine demand for the token. Investors should understand the reasons behind such actions and consider them as part of a broader strategy when evaluating a project's potential.

# Crypto Bites: Snack-sized Insights for the Modern Investor

Chapter 12: Security

Cryptocurrency Exchange Security

Exchange Vulnerabilities:

Cryptocurrency exchanges, both centralized (CEX) and decentralized (DEX), have inherent vulnerabilities. CEXs operate as centralized entities holding vast amounts of user funds, making them lucrative targets for hackers. DEXs, while not holding user funds directly, can have vulnerabilities in their smart contract code that, if exploited, can lead to significant losses.

Historical Hacks:

Several high-profile hacks have jolted the crypto community:

- *Mt. Gox (2014)*: Once handling 70% of all Bitcoin transactions, Mt. Gox lost 850,000 Bitcoins to hackers. It remains one of the largest and most infamous crypto exchange hacks, leading to its eventual bankruptcy.
- *Bitfinex (2016)*: Attackers exploited vulnerabilities to drain 120,000 Bitcoins, equivalent to $72 million at the time.
- *DAO Attack on Ethereum (2016)*: A DEX's faulty smart contract code was manipulated, resulting in the theft of $60 million worth of Ether and a controversial blockchain split to revert the theft.

Bolstering Security:

Post these incidents, exchanges have amped up security. They now invest in regular security audits, penetration testing, and employ multi-signature wallets which require multiple private keys to authorize a transaction, making a breach less likely.

Security Features for Users:

- *Two-Factor Authentication (2FA)*: This requires users to provide two types of identification before accessing their accounts, adding an extra layer of security.
- *Withdrawal Whitelists*: Users can set specific addresses as the only destinations for withdrawals, preventing unauthorized fund transfers to unknown addresses.

Conclusion: Exchange security has undeniably evolved following the lessons of past breaches. While risks persist, awareness, and the implementation of advanced security measures make today's crypto trading far more secure than in the early days of the industry. Users, too, have a role in ensuring their funds' safety by leveraging available security tools.

# Crypto Bites: Snack-sized Insights for the Modern Investor

Phishing Attacks and Social Engineering

Phishing attacks and social engineering are manipulative tactics cybercriminals use to deceive individuals into divulging sensitive information. As the digital age progresses, these schemes have become increasingly sophisticated, targeting unsuspecting victims in the cryptocurrency and broader financial sectors.

Tactics:

- *Phishing Websites*: These are counterfeit websites mimicking legitimate platforms. An unsuspecting user might input their login details, thinking they're accessing a trusted site, only to have their information captured by the attacker.
- *Email Scams*: Fraudulent emails pretending to be from reputable sources encourage users to click on embedded links leading to phishing sites or to download malware. These emails often create a sense of urgency or promise rewards.
- *Fake Support Agents*: Malicious actors may pose as customer support agents, often on social media, directing users to phishing sites or convincing them to share private keys or passwords.

Recognizing Threats:

- Check URLs carefully for slight misspellings or different domain extensions (e.g., .net instead of .com).
- Hover over links in emails to preview the destination URL without clicking.
- Be wary of unsolicited communications requesting urgent actions or personal data.
- Use official channels for support, avoiding random social media accounts or unverified phone numbers.

Precautions:

- Always enable two-factor authentication (2FA) for accounts.
- Regularly update and patch software to protect against known vulnerabilities.
- Use antivirus and anti-phishing toolbars to detect and block threats.
- Never share private keys, passwords, or pin codes.

Conclusion:

While the digital realm offers immense benefits, it's also riddled with pitfalls designed by malicious actors. Awareness, constant vigilance, and adopting best practices are crucial to navigating this space safely. Being informed about the tactics and tricks of scammers is the first line of defense against potential loss.

Wallet Security - Private Key Protection

In the realm of cryptocurrencies, owning your private key means owning your funds. The private key is a cryptographic element that allows users to access and manage their digital assets. Ensuring its protection is paramount for securing one's holdings.

1. The Sanctity of the Private Key:

The private key is a unique string of characters that grants access to the assets stored in a cryptocurrency wallet. If someone else gains access to this key, they can transfer or spend your funds. Hence, it's often said: "Not your keys, not your coins." This underscores the importance of maintaining the confidentiality of the private key at all times.

2. Custodial vs. Non-Custodial Wallets:

- *Custodial Wallets*: These are held by third parties, such as exchanges. While they handle security, they also retain control of your private keys, meaning users rely on the platform's security measures and trust.
- *Non-Custodial Wallets*: Users control their private keys directly. While this offers more control and eliminates third-party risks, it places the onus of security entirely on the user.

3. Best Practices for Key Storage:

- Cold Storage: Keeping a private key offline, away from internet access, mitigates the risk of online hacks. This can be achieved using paper wallets or hardware wallets.
- Hardware Wallets: Devices like the Ledger Nano S or Trezor provide a secure environment for private key storage, isolated from online threats. Transactions can be signed within the device, ensuring the private key never exposes itself online.
- Backup: Always maintain multiple backups of the private key in secure locations. A lost key can mean a permanent loss of assets.

4. Conclusion:

Private key protection is the bedrock of cryptocurrency security. While the ecosystem offers numerous tools and practices to safeguard these keys, users must remain informed and vigilant to keep their digital assets secure.

# Crypto Bites: Snack-sized Insights for the Modern Investor

Smart Contract Vulnerabilities

Smart contracts, while revolutionary in automating and verifying transactions on blockchain platforms, are not exempt from potential pitfalls. As pieces of code, they are susceptible to vulnerabilities that, if exploited, can lead to considerable financial losses.

Noteworthy Incidents:

The most infamous case is the *DAO hack*. The DAO (Decentralized Autonomous Organization) aimed to operate as a leaderless venture capital fund on Ethereum. Due to a vulnerability in its code, an attacker drained around 3.6 million Ether, which led to drastic measures, including a contentious hard fork in Ethereum to reverse the theft.

Common Vulnerabilities:

- Reentrancy Attacks: This happens when, within a single transaction, the same function is entered multiple times before the first function execution is completed. In the DAO's case, this allowed the hacker to repetitively withdraw funds.
- Underflows and Overflows: These are tied to numeric boundaries in computational systems. Overflow happens when a number exceeds its variable limit, making it reset to a minimum value, and underflow is the opposite. Malicious actors can exploit these if they're not appropriately checked.

Importance of Security:

- Contract Audits: Critical to ensure a smart contract's security, professional audits can identify and rectify vulnerabilities before deployment.
- Secure Coding: Adhering to best practices in coding can prevent many vulnerabilities. Utilizing updated versions of programming languages like Solidity and being aware of its quirks is essential.
- Community Vigilance: Open-source nature means that the community can review and identify potential threats. Taking feedback seriously and acting on it promptly ensures resilience.

In Conclusion:

Smart contracts carry the promise of trustless, automated transactions. However, their integrity depends on robust security measures, regular audits, and a vigilant community. Ensuring these can maintain trust and deter potential vulnerabilities.

# Crypto Bites: Snack-sized Insights for the Modern Investor

General Digital Hygiene and Best Practices

Navigating the digital landscape, especially within the cryptocurrency realm, demands a proactive approach to security. With the irreversible nature of crypto transactions and the growing sophistication of malicious actors, adhering to digital hygiene best practices is not optional; it's essential. Here's a summary of core habits every crypto enthusiast should integrate:

1. Regular Software Updates:
   o Why It's Important: Software updates often include patches for known vulnerabilities. Running outdated software can expose you to risks.
   o Best Practice: Regularly update your operating system, wallet software, and any related apps. Ensure updates come from legitimate sources.
2. Secure & Unique Passwords:
   o Why It's Important: Passwords are often the first line of defense. Using weak or repetitive passwords makes you an easy target.
   o Best Practice: Use password managers to generate and store complex passwords. Never reuse passwords across platforms.
3. Two-Factor Authentication (2FA):
   o Why It's Important: 2FA adds an extra layer of security, requiring both something you know (password) and something you have (e.g., a mobile device or hardware token).
   o Best Practice: Enable 2FA on all platforms, especially crypto exchanges and wallets. Preferably use hardware-based or app-based 2FA rather than SMS.
4. Beware of Unsolicited Communications:
   o Why It's Important: Phishing attempts often come as unsolicited emails, messages, or calls that prompt action, like clicking on a link.
   o Best Practice: Always verify the source. Avoid clicking on unexpected links or downloading attachments. When in doubt, contact the service provider directly through official channels.
5. Too-Good-To-Be-True Offers:
   o Why It's Important: Scammers lure victims with promises of high returns or "free" money.
   o Best Practice: Exercise skepticism. If an offer seems too lucrative or requires upfront payments, it's likely a scam.

In essence, good digital hygiene is a blend of common sense, knowledge, and habitual caution. Regularly revisiting and updating these practices is vital to remain secure in an ever-evolving digital landscape.

Chapter 13: Risks

Volatility and Market Dynamics in the Crypto Space

The cryptocurrency market, known for its rapid price swings, has gained a reputation for being highly volatile. This volatility can be attributed to a myriad of factors, and while it presents opportunities for significant gains, it also comes with considerable risks.

Factors Contributing to Volatility:

1. News-Driven Events: Crypto prices are especially sensitive to news and regulatory announcements. Positive news, like a country's acceptance of a cryptocurrency or a major corporation investing in Bitcoin, can lead to bullish runs. Conversely, reports of regulatory crackdowns, security breaches, or negative sentiments from influential figures can send prices tumbling.
2. Market Sentiment: The crypto market, still in its adolescence, is highly influenced by retail investor sentiment. Hype, fear of missing out (FOMO), or conversely, panic selling, can lead to sudden and large-scale price movements.
3. Whales' Actions: 'Whales,' or large holders of cryptocurrencies, have the power to move the market. A significant transaction or a series of transactions by a whale can create ripples throughout the market, pushing prices up or down.
4. Liquidity Concerns: In some cases, especially with less popular tokens, low liquidity can lead to exaggerated price fluctuations. With fewer tokens available to trade, even small trades can have a disproportionate impact on price.

The Double-Edged Nature of Volatility:

For traders and investors, the volatility in the crypto market offers a chance for high returns. Rapid price increases can result in significant profits in a short time frame. However, the same volatility also poses risks. Sharp downturns can lead to substantial losses, and the unpredictable nature of the market can make it challenging to time trades effectively.

In conclusion, understanding the volatile nature of the crypto market is crucial for anyone looking to invest or trade. While the potential for profit is alluring, it's equally vital to be aware of the inherent risks and to approach the market with caution and informed decision-making.

Notes: _____

_____

_____

# Crypto Bites: Snack-sized Insights for the Modern Investor

Regulatory Uncertainties and Geopolitical Influences on Cryptocurrencies

Cryptocurrencies, once the purview of tech enthusiasts, have grown into a significant global financial phenomenon. However, with this growth comes increased regulatory scrutiny, which plays a crucial role in shaping the market dynamics of this burgeoning industry.

Regulatory Changes and Market Impact:

1. Major Jurisdictions' Influence: When key countries or regions announce or adjust their regulatory stance on cryptocurrencies, it can send ripples through the global market. For instance, when the U.S. SEC makes statements about potential regulations or when the European Union discusses standardizing crypto laws, such news can immediately influence market sentiment, leading to price fluctuations.
2. Regulatory Clarity vs. Uncertainty: Positive regulatory news, like clear guidelines or acceptance of crypto practices, often boosts market confidence, leading to bullish trends. In contrast, ambiguous or negative regulatory stances can create uncertainty, leading to bearish market responses. A well-defined regulatory environment can foster innovation and attract institutional investors, further stabilizing the market.

Geopolitical Risks:

1. Bans and Restrictions: Some nations, concerned about the potential implications of decentralized currencies on their economic systems or national security, have outright banned or restricted crypto activities. These bans can lead to sharp declines in global cryptocurrency adoption rates and prices.
2. Government Crackdowns: In some regions, governments have initiated crackdowns on crypto mining activities, citing environmental concerns or potential power shortages. Such actions can influence the supply dynamics of cryptocurrencies, especially Bitcoin, and thus their prices.
3. Geopolitical Tensions: Cryptocurrencies might be viewed as alternative financial systems or tools during geopolitical crises. In instances of economic sanctions, countries might look to cryptos as potential bypass mechanisms, influencing demand.

In conclusion, the relationship between cryptocurrencies and regulatory/geopolitical influences is a delicate dance. While regulatory clarity can foster growth and adoption, uncertainties and geopolitical tensions present challenges that investors and participants need to navigate. Being aware of these dynamics is crucial for understanding the broader crypto ecosystem's trajectory.

# Crypto Bites: Snack-sized Insights for the Modern Investor

Technological Vulnerabilities in Crypto Investments

Cryptocurrencies, while heralded for their decentralized and secure nature, are not immune to technological vulnerabilities. Several technical risks could potentially compromise the safety and value of one's crypto investments.

1. Blockchain Network Vulnerabilities:

- 51% Attacks: Predominantly a risk for smaller, less secure blockchains, a 51% attack occurs when a single entity controls over half the network's mining power. This dominance allows them to double-spend coins and halt transactions, undermining the integrity of that blockchain.

- Sybil Attacks: In a Sybil attack, a single adversary controls multiple nodes in a network, primarily to spread misinformation. Decentralized networks like blockchain are designed to resist such attacks, but the threat remains, especially in younger, less developed networks.

2. Smart Contract Bugs:

- Smart contracts are self-executing contracts with the agreement directly written into code. As code, they can contain bugs or vulnerabilities. If exploited, these bugs can lead to significant financial losses, as was the case with the DAO hack in 2016.

3. Wallet Security Risks:

- Cryptocurrency wallets, both hot (online) and cold (offline), can be vulnerable. Hot wallets are susceptible to hacking, phishing, and malware attacks. Cold wallets, while safer from online threats, can be lost or damaged.

4. Quantum Computing Threats:

- Quantum computers, with their vastly superior processing capabilities, pose a theoretical risk to cryptographic systems underpinning blockchains. They might be able to break cryptographic protections faster than conventional computers, though the technology is still nascent.

5. Evolution of Blockchain Solutions:

- As threats arise, the crypto community continually innovates. Layered security protocols, off-chain scaling solutions, and quantum-resistant cryptographic algorithms are being developed to counteract vulnerabilities.

# Crypto Bites: Snack-sized Insights for the Modern Investor

Operational and Counterparty Risks in Cryptocurrency

The cryptocurrency ecosystem, while revolutionizing traditional finance, introduces its own set of operational and counterparty risks that investors and participants must be keenly aware of.

1. Operational Risks with Crypto Platforms:

- Exchange Vulnerabilities: Crypto exchanges, being digital and often holding large sums of assets, become lucrative targets for cybercriminals. Notable hacks, like the Mt. Gox incident in 2014 and the Coincheck heist in 2018, resulted in the loss of hundreds of millions of dollars.
- Wallet Risks: While wallets are designed to securely store crypto, they too can be vulnerable. Software wallets can be hacked, and hardware wallets can be physically lost or damaged.
- Due Diligence: With the proliferation of crypto platforms, ensuring the legitimacy and security of an exchange or wallet is crucial. Researching platform reviews, checking for regulatory compliance, and evaluating security protocols is imperative.
- Centralized Platforms: Storing large amounts of cryptocurrency on centralized platforms exposes users to heightened risk. Centralized exchanges can be compromised, or they could face liquidity issues, leaving users unable to access their funds.

2. Counterparty Risks in Decentralized Protocols:

- Smart Contract Failures: In decentralized finance (DeFi) platforms, smart contracts facilitate lending, borrowing, and other financial actions. If these contracts have vulnerabilities or bugs, they can be exploited, leading to financial losses.
- Liquidity Risks: Some DeFi platforms depend on user deposits for liquidity. Should many users withdraw simultaneously or if a "bank run" occurs, it might be challenging to retrieve funds.
- Impermanent Loss: In decentralized liquidity pools, asset value fluctuations can result in impermanent loss, where providing liquidity becomes less profitable than merely holding the assets.

In summation, while cryptocurrencies offer a novel approach to finance and investment, they come with distinct operational and counterparty risks. Awareness, due diligence, and cautious participation are key to navigating these potential pitfalls.

Chapter 14: Regulation and Compliance

The Regulatory Landscape - A Global Overview

The global regulatory landscape for cryptocurrencies is diverse and ever-evolving, with nations adopting a range of approaches that impact global adoption, innovation, and market dynamics.

1. Permissive Frameworks:

- Examples: Switzerland, Singapore, and Malta.
- Characteristics: These jurisdictions often provide clear and supportive regulatory environments. They might offer guidelines for ICOs, tax incentives, or favorable banking relationships for crypto businesses.
- Impacts: Such frameworks can attract blockchain startups, fostering innovation hubs and drawing international investments.

2. Moderate Regulation:

- Examples: The United States, Canada, and several European Union countries.
- Characteristics: These nations often strike a balance. While they don't clamp down on crypto activities, they do implement regulations to curb illicit activities and protect investors. The U.S., for instance, has been cautious, with the SEC providing guidelines on token offerings and considering certain tokens as securities.
- Impacts: This balanced approach gives a level of security to investors and users while still allowing room for growth and innovation in the sector.

3. Restrictive Stances:

- Examples: China and India.
- Characteristics: Some countries adopt a skeptical view. China, for instance, has imposed bans on ICOs, crypto exchanges, and recently, crypto mining. India has also vacillated on its regulatory approach, causing uncertainty.
- Impacts: Such stances can stifle local innovation and push entrepreneurs and investors to more crypto-friendly jurisdictions. However, despite these restrictions, underground or decentralized activities can still persist.

4. Outright Bans:

- Examples: Morocco and Bangladesh.
- Characteristics: Few countries have taken steps to completely ban the use, trading, or possession of cryptocurrencies.

# Crypto Bites: Snack-sized Insights for the Modern Investor

- Impacts: These bans often arise from concerns about financial stability, illicit activities, or loss of control over monetary policy. Yet, such strict measures can hinder technological progress and might not always curb underground crypto activities.

Conclusion: The global crypto regulatory landscape is a mosaic of approaches, each with its implications. As cryptocurrency becomes more integrated into mainstream finance and daily life, the challenge for regulators worldwide will be to protect consumers while not stifling innovation.

Notes: _____

_____

_____

KYC and AML Protocols in Crypto

1. Significance:

*KYC (Know Your Customer)* and *AML (Anti-Money Laundering)* protocols serve as critical components in the modern financial ecosystem, including the crypto sector. Their primary goal is to prevent identity theft, financial fraud, and the illicit transfer of funds, such as money laundering or financing terrorism.

2. Implementation in Crypto:

- Exchanges: Most centralized exchanges (e.g., Coinbase, Binance, and Kraken) require users to undergo a KYC process. This typically involves providing personal information, proof of address, and a photo ID. Some exchanges also utilize biometric verification methods, like facial recognition.
- Wallet Providers: While standalone cryptocurrency wallets (especially hardware or paper wallets) might not necessitate KYC checks, certain online wallet providers or wallets linked to exchange platforms might require some level of KYC, especially if they facilitate fiat-to-crypto transactions.

3. Implications for User Privacy:

- Pros: KYC and AML measures can add a layer of security, ensuring that a user's account is harder to compromise. It can also aid in the recovery of accounts if issues arise.
- Cons: The need to share personal information goes against the grain of the "pseudonymous" nature of cryptocurrencies. This can lead to privacy concerns, especially if the platform's security is breached. Furthermore, there's a potential for misuse of data or surveillance by authorities.

4. Implications for Security:

- Pros: By ensuring that users are verified, exchanges can safeguard against malicious actors, thus enhancing the platform's overall security and integrity.
- Cons: Centralized data storage creates 'honey pots' of information, which can be attractive targets for hackers. Breaches could result in the exposure of sensitive user information.

Conclusion: While KYC and AML protocols in the crypto sector are essential for aligning with global financial regulations and ensuring platform security, they come with trade-offs regarding user privacy. As the crypto industry matures, finding a balance between regulation, security, and user privacy will remain a pivotal challenge.

# Crypto Bites: Snack-sized Insights for the Modern Investor

Securities and Cryptocurrencies

## 1. The Debate:

Cryptocurrencies, in their myriad forms, have spurred significant debate regarding their classification. One of the central discussions revolves around whether certain cryptocurrencies or ICOs can be categorized as "securities." Such classification has profound implications for how these assets are regulated, promoted, and sold.

## 2. Criteria by Regulatory Entities:

The U.S. Securities and Exchange Commission (SEC) utilizes the "Howey Test" to determine if a transaction qualifies as an investment contract (i.e., a type of security). For an ICO or a cryptocurrency to be a security, it must meet the following criteria:

- Investment of Money: There is an investment of money or assets.
- Expectation of Profits: Investors expect to profit from the investment.
- Common Enterprise: The investment is in a common enterprise.
- Profits Derived from the Efforts of Others: Profit comes mainly from the efforts of a promoter or third party.

## 3. Implications for Projects Deemed to be Securities:

- Regulatory Compliance: Projects that are classified as securities must register with the SEC, disclose specific financial information, and adhere to regulations, unless they qualify for an exemption.
- Increased Scrutiny: These projects come under increased regulatory scrutiny, with potential penalties for non-compliance.
- Operational Challenges: Being classified as a security can limit a project's ability to be listed on certain exchanges, restrict promotional activities, and could necessitate additional legal and advisory expenses.
- Investor Perception: The classification might impact investor sentiment, as some might view them as more legitimate, while others might see increased regulatory challenges.

Conclusion: The intersection of cryptocurrencies and securities law is a dynamic space. While regulatory clarity can help foster innovation, it can also pose challenges. Projects must be vigilant in understanding and navigating the evolving regulatory landscape to ensure compliance and protect stakeholders.

# Crypto Bites: Snack-sized Insights for the Modern Investor

Taxation and Cryptocurrencies

1. The Evolving Landscape:

Cryptocurrency taxation is an evolving domain, with many jurisdictions formulating and refining their stance as the sector grows. Understanding tax implications is vital for crypto enthusiasts to ensure compliance and avoid potential penalties.

2. Taxable Events:

Several events can trigger a tax liability in the realm of cryptocurrencies:

- Trading: Selling cryptocurrencies for fiat or exchanging one cryptocurrency for another can be considered a taxable event, often triggering capital gains or losses.
- Mining: Earning crypto through mining can be treated as income at its fair market value when received. Subsequent sales can also lead to capital gains or losses.
- Earning Crypto: Receiving cryptocurrencies for services rendered or through mechanisms like staking, airdrops, or interest can be taxable, generally considered as ordinary income.

3. Jurisdictional Differences:

Tax treatment varies by jurisdiction. Some classify crypto as property, invoking capital gains tax, while others may treat it as currency or even a commodity. Certain jurisdictions offer tax-friendly policies, with exemptions on long-held assets, while others may be stricter with comprehensive reporting requirements.

4. Challenges in Reporting:

The decentralized and sometimes pseudonymous nature of crypto transactions can make reporting complex. Tracking cost basis, especially for those with multiple transactions across various platforms, can be intricate. Ensuring accurate records of all transactions, including dates, amounts, and prices, is imperative.

5. Tools for Compliance:

Various software tools and platforms have emerged to assist users in crypto tax reporting. These tools can aggregate transaction data across multiple exchanges, calculate gains or losses, and generate tax reports compliant with local regulations.

Conclusion: Navigating the world of cryptocurrency taxation requires a blend of diligence and awareness of local regulations. As regulatory clarity emerges, staying informed and prepared is the best strategy for crypto participants.

Future of Crypto Regulation

1. The Evolving Landscape:

As cryptocurrencies transition from a niche novelty to an integrated component of the global financial system, regulatory clarity becomes imperative. While the early days of crypto were marked by a "Wild West" mentality, we are now observing increased efforts by governments to understand, regulate, and harness this technology.

2. Global Regulatory Alignment:

Given the borderless nature of cryptocurrencies, there's a growing sentiment for a harmonized global regulatory framework. Institutions like the G20 have already started discussing broad guidelines. While it's unlikely that a one-size-fits-all approach will emerge given the diverse priorities of nations, we may see more standardized rules around key areas such as Anti-Money Laundering (AML) and Counter Financing of Terrorism (CFT).

3. Emerging Standards:

As the industry matures, we might witness the introduction of global standards, particularly in areas like security, consumer protection, and interoperability. These standards would not only protect users but also ensure smoother interaction between different crypto systems and traditional finance.

4. Evolving Governmental Attitudes:

Initial hesitance or resistance to cryptocurrencies by governments might evolve into acceptance or even endorsement. Some nations might adopt or issue their own digital currencies, or "Central Bank Digital Currencies" (CBDCs), which could co-exist alongside decentralized crypto assets.

5. Integration into Mainstream Finance:

Regulatory clarity can pave the way for greater institutional participation. Traditional banks and financial entities might offer crypto services, fostering trust and further adoption among the masses.

Conclusion: While predicting the exact trajectory of crypto regulation is challenging, it's evident that the sector is transitioning from its anarchic roots towards a more structured and regulated future. This evolution, if executed judiciously, can ensure that the revolutionary potential of cryptocurrencies is realized while mitigating associated risks.

Chapter 15: Tax Implications

Taxable Crypto Events:

Cryptocurrencies have not only introduced a new mode of value exchange but have also brought forth intricate tax implications. While regulations differ globally, certain crypto events consistently create taxable situations.

1. Selling Cryptocurrencies for Fiat: When you sell a cryptocurrency and convert it into a fiat currency (like USD, EUR, or any local currency), it typically triggers a taxable event. The tax owed is calculated based on the capital gains or losses from the sale, determined by the difference between the sale price and the initial purchase price.

2. Crypto-to-Crypto Trades: In many jurisdictions, trading one cryptocurrency for another — say, Bitcoin for Ethereum — is considered a taxable event. Even if no fiat is involved, capital gains or losses need to be reported for each trade.

3. Mined Cryptocurrencies: If you mine cryptocurrencies, the mined coins might be considered income at their fair market value when received. This becomes the cost basis for any future sales or trades, leading to capital gains or losses.

4. Earnings from Staking or DeFi: Earning cryptocurrencies through staking or participating in DeFi platforms can also be taxable. The earned assets may be treated as income, depending on the jurisdiction, and could also have future tax implications when they are sold or traded.

5. Capital Gains: Short-term vs. Long-term: Cryptocurrencies held for less than a year (or a specific period depending on local regulations) before selling or trading typically incur short-term capital gains tax. Conversely, assets held for longer durations fall under long-term capital gains, which often have different tax rates.

In essence, most interactions with cryptocurrencies have potential tax implications. It's crucial for participants to maintain detailed records and seek guidance from tax professionals familiar with local crypto regulations.

Notes: _____

_____

_____

Crypto Losses and Tax Deductions

Cryptocurrencies can be as unpredictable as they are innovative, and just as there are opportunities for significant gains, there are also chances of substantial losses. For many crypto investors, understanding how these losses interact with taxation can be pivotal.

1. Offsetting Gains with Losses: In the world of taxes, capital losses—those losses incurred upon selling an asset for less than the purchase price—can often be utilized to counterbalance capital gains. For instance, if an investor realizes a gain from selling a particular cryptocurrency but incurs a loss in another, this loss can be used to offset the gain, reducing the overall taxable amount.

2. "Wash Sale" Rules: Certain jurisdictions employ "wash sale" rules, which prevent investors from claiming a loss on a sale of an asset if they buy a "substantially identical" asset within 30 days before or after the sale. While these rules traditionally apply to stocks and securities, their applicability to cryptocurrencies varies by jurisdiction. As of my last update, the U.S., for instance, hadn't formally applied the wash sale rule to crypto, but this could change.

3. Carrying Forward Losses: In some tax systems, if your capital losses exceed your capital gains for the year, you can carry forward these losses to offset future gains or even ordinary income, depending on limits set by local regulations.

4. Record-Keeping is Crucial: Given the complex nature of crypto transactions and the importance of accurate tax reporting, meticulous record-keeping is essential. Investors should maintain records of transaction dates, amounts, and prices, as well as any receipts, to substantiate their deduction claims.

In sum, while facing a loss in the crypto sphere can be disappointing, the silver lining lies in potential tax deductions. Always consult with a tax professional to navigate the nuances of your jurisdiction's crypto tax landscape.

Notes: _____

_____

_____

International Considerations and Reporting Obligations

The world of cryptocurrency, by its very nature, is borderless. Yet, as global as the crypto ecosystem might be, tax regulations remain predominantly local. This dichotomy presents unique challenges and complexities for crypto users operating across international boundaries.

1. Foreign Exchanges and Tax Implications: Engaging with a cryptocurrency exchange based in a foreign country might necessitate additional reporting. For instance, U.S. citizens are required to report foreign financial accounts through the FBAR if the total value exceeds $10,000 at any point during the calendar year.

2. The Peril of Double Taxation: Given that different countries have varying taxation frameworks for cryptocurrencies, an international crypto transaction might result in double taxation. While tax treaties might provide relief in some cases, the nascent nature of crypto regulations means many nuances are yet to be addressed.

3. Reporting Foreign Assets: Some jurisdictions mandate the reporting of foreign-held assets beyond just bank accounts. For U.S. taxpayers, this might mean complying with FATCA, which requires the declaration of certain foreign assets, potentially including cryptocurrencies.

4. The Common Reporting Standard (CRS): Initiated by the OECD, the CRS seeks to combat tax evasion through an automatic exchange of financial account information between countries. For crypto holders, this could mean their account data on foreign platforms might be shared with their home country's tax authorities.

In conclusion, while cryptocurrencies offer an unprecedented level of financial freedom and global operability, they come with intricate international tax and reporting responsibilities. It's imperative for international crypto users to stay informed and ideally, seek advice from tax professionals familiar with the crypto space across jurisdictions.

Notes: _____

_____

_____

Chapter 16: Initial Coin Offerings (ICOs) and Token Sales

Understanding ICOs: Basics and Mechanisms

At the intersection of blockchain innovation and fundraising, Initial Coin Offerings (ICOs) have charted a disruptive path, enabling startups to raise vast amounts swiftly. Let's unpack the foundational aspects of ICOs:

1. What is an ICO?:
    o An ICO, at its core, is a fundraising method where new projects sell their underlying crypto tokens to investors in exchange for established cryptocurrencies like Bitcoin or Ethereum. It's analogous to an IPO in the stock market, but without the equity ownership for investors.
2. Historical Context:
    o The concept of ICOs gained traction around 2014, with Ethereum's ICO being a noteworthy success, raising over $18 million. This method emerged as an alternative to traditional venture capital, offering swifter funds and direct access to a global pool of investors.
3. The ICO Process:
    o Pre-sale Phase: Often restricted to private investors or early supporters, this phase offers tokens at a discounted rate before the public sale.
    o Public Sale: The main event where tokens are available to the general public. It can be time-limited or cap-limited, ending when the maximum funding target is reached.
4. Critical ICO Components:
    o Whitepapers: The bedrock of any ICO, a whitepaper details the project's purpose, technology, tokenomics, and more. It's the project's blueprint, giving potential investors insight into its viability.
    o Tokenomics: A study of the token's economic model. It answers questions like: How many tokens will exist? What's their purpose? How will they be distributed?
    o Roadmaps: A project's developmental timeline, indicating its vision, milestones, and future plans.

In summation, ICOs present a radical shift in fundraising dynamics. However, with vast potential also come risks, making it essential for investors to comprehend the mechanism, utility, and the team behind the venture.

Notes: _____

_____

_____

Regulatory Landscape and Challenges for ICOs

The surge of Initial Coin Offerings (ICOs) didn't just catch the attention of investors; it also rang alarm bells for regulators worldwide. With a blend of innovation and risk, the regulatory approach to ICOs has been a blend of caution, scrutiny, and attempts to fit a novel model into traditional frameworks.

1.  Token Classifications:
    o   Utility Tokens: These tokens grant holders access to a specific product or service on a platform. Ideally, they aren't designed for investment but rather for future use in a platform or ecosystem.
    o   Security Tokens: Echoing traditional securities, these tokens derive their value from an external asset or promise of future profits. They're subjected to rigorous securities regulations in many jurisdictions.

The distinction is pivotal. If a token is deemed a security but hasn't followed security-offering regulations, the issuing organization might face severe legal repercussions.

2.  The U.S. Regulatory Approach:
    o   SEC's Stance: The U.S. Securities and Exchange Commission (SEC) has been at the forefront, with a cautious stance on ICOs. Their notable action against projects like Telegram and Block.one underscores their commitment to applying traditional securities laws to ICOs.
    o   Guidelines and Clarifications: The SEC has strived to provide clarity, albeit slowly. They've affirmed that while not all tokens are securities, many ICOs fit the bill, especially when they resemble traditional investment contracts.
3.  Global Challenges:
    o   Different countries have varied stances, from outright bans to welcoming frameworks. This disparity makes it challenging for global projects to ensure compliance everywhere.
    o   The evolving nature of crypto projects means that a token starting as a utility might evolve into a security, muddying regulatory waters.

In essence, the ICO regulatory landscape remains in flux. As the crypto domain matures, one can hope for clearer, more harmonized regulations that protect investors without stifling innovation.

Notes: _____

_____

_____

Evaluating ICOs: Risks and Due Diligence

Initial Coin Offerings (ICOs) have revolutionized startup fundraising, bypassing traditional venture capital routes. However, the ICO landscape is rife with high rewards and equally high risks. With numerous projects ranging from revolutionary to fraudulent, conducting due diligence becomes paramount.

1. Red Flags in ICOs:
    o Vague Whitepapers: A project's whitepaper is its foundational document. If it lacks clear objectives, technical details, or is riddled with jargon without substance, caution is warranted.
    o Anonymous Teams: Trustworthy projects proudly display their team, boasting their qualifications and past achievements. A hidden team can be a sign of a lack of accountability or credibility.
    o Unrealistic Promises: "Too good to be true" often holds. Projects claiming guaranteed returns or making lofty promises without concrete plans are suspect.
2. Due Diligence Checklist:
    o Project's Feasibility: Is the project solving a genuine problem? Is its solution technically and economically viable? Consider the competition and the uniqueness of the proposal.
    o Token Utility: Tokens should have a clear purpose within the ecosystem, not just as a fundraising tool. Examine if they're essential for the platform's functionality or if they offer any real advantages.
    o Team's Track Record: A reputable team with a history of achievements in blockchain or related fields is a strong indicator of a project's legitimacy.
    o Community Engagement: A vibrant, engaged community can be a testament to a project's credibility and momentum. Check forums, social media channels, and other platforms for genuine user engagement.

In conclusion, while ICOs present tremendous investment opportunities, they're also fraught with risks. Comprehensive research, critical evaluation, and always following the principle of "buyer beware" can mitigate potential pitfalls and guide investors towards more informed decisions.

Notes: _____

_____

_____

# Crypto Bites: Snack-sized Insights for the Modern Investor

Post-ICO Evolution: From IEOs to IDOs

The Initial Coin Offering (ICO) wave marked a dynamic era in crypto-based fundraising. As the ecosystem evolved and sought more trustworthy and efficient mechanisms, two noteworthy models emerged: Initial Exchange Offerings (IEOs) and Initial DEX Offerings (IDOs).

1. Initial Exchange Offerings (IEOs):
   - Definition: An IEO is a fundraising event where a new cryptocurrency project sells its tokens directly on a crypto exchange platform.
   - Role of Exchanges: Unlike ICOs, where projects directly approached investors, IEOs leverage exchanges as intermediaries. Exchanges vet the projects, reducing the risk of scams.
   - Benefits: Using exchanges as a platform provides instant liquidity upon listing. Investors trust the due diligence done by exchanges, making the IEO process more credible than the earlier ICOs.
   - Limitations: Centralization is a concern, as exchanges hold significant sway over the projects' success. There are also listing fees and the potential for biased selection.
2. Initial DEX Offerings (IDOs):
   - Definition: An IDO occurs when a project launches a token through a decentralized liquidity exchange.
   - Decentralized Nature: Unlike IEOs, IDOs occur on decentralized platforms like Uniswap or Sushiswap. This ensures more democratic access, as tokens are immediately available to anyone using the DEX.
   - Benefits: Low listing fees, immediate liquidity, and open access make IDOs attractive. The decentralized nature also aligns with the ethos of many crypto projects.
   - Limitations: The absence of a centralized authority means less vetting, which can raise concerns about project credibility.

In summary, as the crypto space has matured, fundraising methods have evolved, shifting from the wild west of ICOs to the more structured IEOs and the decentralized IDOs. Each model offers a unique blend of benefits and challenges, reflecting the dynamic nature of the cryptocurrency realm.

Notes: _____

_____

_____

Chapter 17: Use Cases

Remittances and Cross-border Transactions

Remittances, or funds sent by migrants back to their home countries, represent significant financial inflows for many countries. Traditional banking and money transfer systems, however, come with high fees and lengthy transaction times, particularly for cross-border remittances. This is where cryptocurrencies step in, offering transformative solutions.

1. Cost-Effective Transactions: Traditional remittance channels, like banks or services like Western Union, often charge substantial fees, which can be especially burdensome for small transaction amounts. Cryptocurrencies, in contrast, enable transfers at a fraction of the cost, making remittances more affordable for users.
2. Speed and Accessibility: Whereas conventional cross-border transactions can take days, cryptocurrency transactions are processed rapidly, often within minutes. Moreover, crypto-based solutions can be accessed from smartphones, catering to regions with limited banking infrastructure but widespread mobile phone usage.
3. Bypassing Inefficiencies: Cryptocurrencies operate outside the traditional banking network, avoiding its bureaucratic layers, currency conversion costs, and the need for intermediaries. This decentralized model ensures that transactions are direct and efficient.

Real-World Impact:

- Philippines: Recognizing the potential of crypto-based remittances, the Philippines has seen a surge in platforms like Coins.ph, which facilitate easy conversion of cryptocurrencies to Philippine pesos. With the country receiving billions in remittances annually, such platforms are making a meaningful difference in the way Filipinos receive money from abroad.
- India: As one of the world's largest recipients of remittances, India stands to benefit immensely from crypto solutions. Platforms like Unocoin and WazirX are simplifying the process, allowing seamless crypto-to-rupee transactions, thereby ensuring faster and cheaper remittances.

In essence, cryptocurrencies are reshaping the remittance landscape, making cross-border transactions swifter, more accessible, and economical. For countries heavily reliant on remittances, this transformation holds profound economic implications.

# Crypto Bites: Snack-sized Insights for the Modern Investor

Decentralized Finance (DeFi) Platforms

Decentralized Finance, commonly known as DeFi, represents a revolutionary shift in the financial sector. Leveraging blockchain technology, DeFi platforms aim to democratize and decentralize traditional financial functions such as lending, borrowing, and trading of derivatives, freeing them from centralized intermediaries.

1. Decentralized Nature: Unlike conventional banking systems where transactions are mediated by banks or financial institutions, DeFi operates on peer-to-peer networks. Smart contracts, self-executing contracts with the agreement terms directly written into code, are pivotal to this, ensuring transactions are trustless and executed without intermediaries.
2. Lending and Borrowing: DeFi platforms enable users to lend or borrow funds directly. Lenders can earn interest by providing liquidity, while borrowers, often providing crypto collateral, can secure loans. This system offers competitive interest rates, driven by supply and demand rather than set by intermediaries.
3. Derivatives and Synthetic Assets: DeFi platforms allow users to create and trade derivatives and synthetic assets, mimicking the value of real-world assets, expanding the reach and possibilities of the crypto domain.

Prominent Examples:

- Compound: A decentralized lending protocol, Compound lets users lend or borrow popular cryptocurrencies. Interest rates are algorithmically adjusted based on supply and demand.
- Aave: Similar to Compound but offering unique features like "flash loans", Aave is another decentralized lending platform with a variety of assets available for lending and borrowing.
- MakerDAO: Renowned for its stablecoin, DAI, which is pegged to the US dollar, MakerDAO allows users to lock up assets as collateral and mint DAI against them. This ensures a decentralized stablecoin free from central control.

In conclusion, DeFi platforms, utilizing the strengths of blockchain, are poised to redefine the financial landscape, offering more open, transparent, and inclusive financial services and products.

Notes: _____

_____

_____

Digital Identity and Privacy

The digital age has amplified concerns around identity theft, data breaches, and privacy violations. Amid these challenges, blockchain and cryptocurrencies emerge as potential solutions, promising secure, immutable, and self-sovereign digital identities.

1. Secure and Immutable: Traditional centralized databases, where user information is stored, are vulnerable to hacks and unauthorized alterations. In contrast, blockchain's decentralized ledger system ensures that once an identity is verified and recorded, it can't be changed without consensus. This robustness shields users from identity theft and fraudulent changes.
2. Self-Sovereign Identity: One of the most transformative aspects of blockchain-based identity is the concept of self-sovereignty. Instead of relying on third parties like governments or corporations to validate identity, individuals control their identity proofs on the blockchain. Users can grant or revoke access to their personal data, making them the sole gatekeepers of their information.
3. Revolutionizing Sectors:
   o Online Services: A self-sovereign identity can eliminate the need for multiple usernames and passwords across websites, simplifying and securing the user experience.
   o E-Commerce: Trust is paramount for online transactions. Blockchain identity verification can ensure both buyers and sellers are genuine, reducing fraud.
   o Voting Systems: One of the most profound applications could be in electoral processes. Blockchain can securely verify voter identities, potentially allowing for tamper-proof online voting, and enhancing democratic participation.

Companies like Civic and uPort are pioneering solutions in this domain, offering blockchain-based identity verification services.

In summary, by placing control of personal data back into the hands of individuals and leveraging the inherent security of the blockchain, the paradigm of digital identity and privacy is on the brink of a groundbreaking transformation.

Notes: _____

_____

_____

# Crypto Bites: Snack-sized Insights for the Modern Investor

Institutional Investment in Cryptocurrencies

The cryptocurrency space, once dominated by individual retail investors, has witnessed a steady influx of institutional players. Hedge funds, pension funds, corporate treasuries, and even insurance companies are now allocating portions of their portfolios to cryptocurrencies, with Bitcoin leading the charge.

Several factors drive this trend:

1. Quest for Uncorrelated Assets: Traditional investment portfolios typically comprise stocks, bonds, and commodities. Cryptocurrencies, especially Bitcoin, have demonstrated a relatively low correlation with these traditional asset classes. This makes them a potentially attractive diversification tool, capable of enhancing portfolio returns while mitigating risks.
2. Inflationary Concerns: With central banks worldwide adopting expansive monetary policies in response to economic crises, concerns about inflation and currency debasement have grown. Bitcoin, often dubbed 'digital gold', is seen by many institutional investors as a hedge against inflation, given its capped supply and decentralized nature.
3. Maturation of the Crypto Ecosystem: Over the past years, the cryptocurrency ecosystem has matured substantially. The advent of sophisticated trading platforms, improved liquidity, enhanced security measures, and the introduction of crypto custodial services has made it easier for institutional investors to participate. Moreover, the regulatory environment, while still evolving, has provided more clarity, further boosting institutional confidence.

Real-world examples include MicroStrategy, a software firm that has aggressively added Bitcoin to its corporate treasury, and Fidelity, which has delved deep into the crypto space with trading and custodial services. Furthermore, the launch of Bitcoin futures on major platforms like the Chicago Mercantile Exchange (CME) has provided institutional players with more familiar tools to engage with the asset class.

In conclusion, the convergence of diversification benefits, inflation hedging characteristics, and a more mature ecosystem has made cryptocurrencies, particularly Bitcoin, an increasingly mainstream institutional investment choice.

Notes: _____

_____

_____

Supply Chain Management and Provenance

Supply chain management involves the oversight of materials, information, and finances as they flow from supplier to manufacturer to wholesaler to retailer to consumer. Traditional supply chains are often marred by inefficiencies, lack of transparency, and fraud. Blockchain technology, underpinned by its decentralized and immutable nature, offers solutions to these challenges.

Blockchain provides a transparent, tamper-proof ledger. Every time a product moves through the supply chain, from raw materials to the final consumer product, that event is recorded on the blockchain. This creates an immutable, timestamped record of every product's journey, ensuring full transparency.

One of the most significant advantages is combating counterfeit goods. Luxury brands, often plagued by fake replicas, can use blockchain to verify authenticity. Each genuine product can be given a unique blockchain-based identifier, which customers can then check to ensure the product's genuineness.

Food safety is another area that benefits. For instance, if a food contamination issue arises, instead of recalling vast amounts of product, companies can pinpoint exactly where in the supply chain the problem occurred and address that specific batch. Walmart, in collaboration with IBM's Food Trust blockchain, has implemented such a system, drastically reducing the time to trace the origin of food items from days to mere seconds.

De Beers, the diamond giant, uses blockchain to track diamonds, ensuring they are conflict-free and authentic. Similarly, Everledger uses blockchain to trace the provenance of valuable items like wine, art, and electronics.

In summary, blockchain's transparency and immutability promise to revolutionize supply chain management, offering improved efficiency, reduced fraud, and enhanced consumer trust.

Notes: _____

_____

_____

## Conclusion: The Digital Frontier Awaits

As we draw this exploration to a close, we recognize the profound revolution brought about by cryptocurrencies, blockchain, and digital assets. These technologies have redefined the concept of value, trust, and decentralization in ways previously unimagined. From the inception of Bitcoin in the aftermath of the 2008 financial crisis to the meteoric rise of DeFi, NFTs, and beyond, we've seen the crypto universe evolve at a staggering pace.

Yet, this space remains in its infancy. The complexities we delved into — regulatory challenges, security considerations, evolving token standards, and the continuous innovation of decentralized platforms — are just the tip of the iceberg. The digital frontier is vast, and the opportunities limitless.

As readers, whether you're enthusiasts, developers, investors, or the curious-minded, remember that with every technological advancement comes responsibility. The decentralized nature of this ecosystem places the onus of safety, knowledge, and discretion squarely on our shoulders. Armed with the insights from this book, we can navigate this world with confidence, ever mindful of the principles of transparency, inclusivity, and community that form the bedrock of the crypto universe.

Looking ahead, we stand on the precipice of a world where the lines between the physical and the digital blur, where technology and humanity converge in harmony. This is not just the future of finance or art or technology; it's the future of interconnected human experience. Embrace it, question it, but most importantly, be part of it. The digital frontier awaits, and the journey has only just begun.

Notes: _____

_____

_____

# Crypto Bites: Snack-sized Insights for the Modern Investor

Essential Resources for Crypto Enthusiasts

Embarking on the journey into the world of cryptocurrencies, blockchain, and decentralized technologies demands a wealth of resources for continuous learning, updates, and networking. This chapter curates some of the most invaluable tools, platforms, and communities to keep you updated, safe, and engaged.

1. Websites for Learning & News:

- CoinDesk: A leading source for crypto news, updates, and market data.
- Cointelegraph: Features the latest blockchain and cryptocurrency news.
- CryptoCompare: For detailed cryptocurrency data, charts, and insights.
- CryptoWisdom.com: For course, books, insight and timely articles, videos and more.

2. Tools & Platforms:

- Metamask: A crypto wallet and gateway to blockchain apps.
- Etherscan: Ethereum blockchain explorer and analytics platform.
- CoinMarketCap: Tracks capitalization of various cryptocurrencies, providing detailed metrics.

3. Forums & Communities:

- BitcoinTalk: The largest and one of the oldest message boards dedicated to blockchain and cryptocurrencies.
- r/CryptoCurrency: A Reddit community for open discussions on all subjects related to emerging crypto and blockchain.

4. Educational Platforms:

- Coursera: Offers comprehensive courses on blockchain, Bitcoin, and cryptocurrencies.
- Udemy: Features a plethora of courses from crypto basics to advanced trading strategies.

5. Security & Protection:

- Have I Been Pwned: Check if your email has been compromised in a data breach.
- 2FA Authenticators: Google Authenticator and Authy provide two-factor authentication, a must-have for added security.

6. Podcasts & Interviews:

- Unchained: Hosted by Laura Shin, this podcast dives deep with industry pioneers.
- The Pomp Podcast: Anthony Pompliano covers the latest in crypto trends and interviews key players.

7. Books:

- "Mastering Bitcoin" by Andreas M. Antonopoulos: A comprehensive guide to understanding Bitcoin.
- "The Age of Cryptocurrency" by Paul Vigna & Michael J. Casey: Delves into how Bitcoin and blockchain technology are challenging the economic order.

8. Conferences & Events:

- Consensus: Organized by CoinDesk, it's one of the most significant blockchain technology gatherings.
- Devcon: Ethereum's annual conference focusing on its development.

Conclusion: While this resource guide offers a starting point, the crypto realm is vast, and evolving daily. Always be on the lookout for new platforms, insights, and communities. Engage actively, be discerning about the information you consume, and most importantly, never stop learning. The world of cryptocurrency, after all, belongs to the curious and the passionate.

Notes: _____

_____

_____

# Crypto Bites: Snack-sized Insights for the Modern Investor

## Glossary of Cryptocurrency and Blockchain Terms

- **Address**: A string of letters and numbers which is used to receive cryptocurrency. Comparable to an account number in traditional banking.
- **Altcoin**: Any cryptocurrency other than Bitcoin.
- **ATH (All-Time High)**: The highest price ever reached by a cryptocurrency.
- **Blockchain**: A decentralized ledger of all transactions across a network, where data is stored in blocks.
- **Cold Storage**: Keeping a reserve of cryptocurrency offline, using methods like paper wallets or hardware wallets.
- **Consensus**: Agreement within a blockchain network on the validity of transactions.
- **Cryptocurrency**: A type of digital or virtual currency that uses cryptography for security.
- **Decentralized**: Not controlled by any single entity or institution.
- **ERC-20, ERC-721, ERC-1155**: Token standards on the Ethereum platform that ensure compatibility between different tokens.
- **Fork**: A split in a blockchain, resulting in two separate chains.
- **FUD (Fear, Uncertainty, Doubt)**: Spreading negative, misleading, or false information to harm a project's reputation.
- **Gas**: A unit that measures the amount of computational effort required to execute Ethereum operations.
- **Halving**: An event where the block reward for mining is divided by two, reducing the rate at which new cryptocurrency is created.
- **Hash**: A function that converts an input into a fixed-length string of characters, which is typically a hash code.
- **Hot Wallet**: A cryptocurrency wallet that is connected to the internet.
- **ICO (Initial Coin Offering)**: A type of crowdfunding using cryptocurrency.
- **Liquidity**: The ability to quickly buy/sell an asset without causing a drastic change in its price.
- **Mining**: The process of validating and recording transactions on a blockchain.
- **Node**: A computer connected to the blockchain network, participating in its functioning.
- **Private Key**: A secret alphanumeric password used to send or spend cryptocurrencies.
- **Public Key**: An alphanumeric code that is shared with others and is used to receive cryptocurrency.
- **Satoshi**: The smallest unit of Bitcoin, equivalent to 0.00000001 BTC.
- **Smart Contract**: A self-executing contract where the agreement between the buyer and seller is written into lines of code.
- **Stablecoin**: A cryptocurrency that pegs its market value to some external reference like the US dollar.
- **Token**: A digital asset issued and traded on a blockchain.

# Crypto Bites: Snack-sized Insights for the Modern Investor

- **Wallet**: A digital tool that allows users to interact with a blockchain, enabling them to send, receive, and manage their cryptocurrency.
- **Whale**: An individual or entity that holds a large amount of cryptocurrency.
- **Yield Farming**: The practice of staking or lending crypto assets to generate high returns.

**Note:** The world of cryptocurrency and blockchain is ever-evolving, and new terms are introduced regularly. This glossary provides a foundational understanding, but always seek to stay updated with the latest terminology and concepts.

Notes: _____

_____

_____